Professional Portfolio 2014

Joseph Fleming

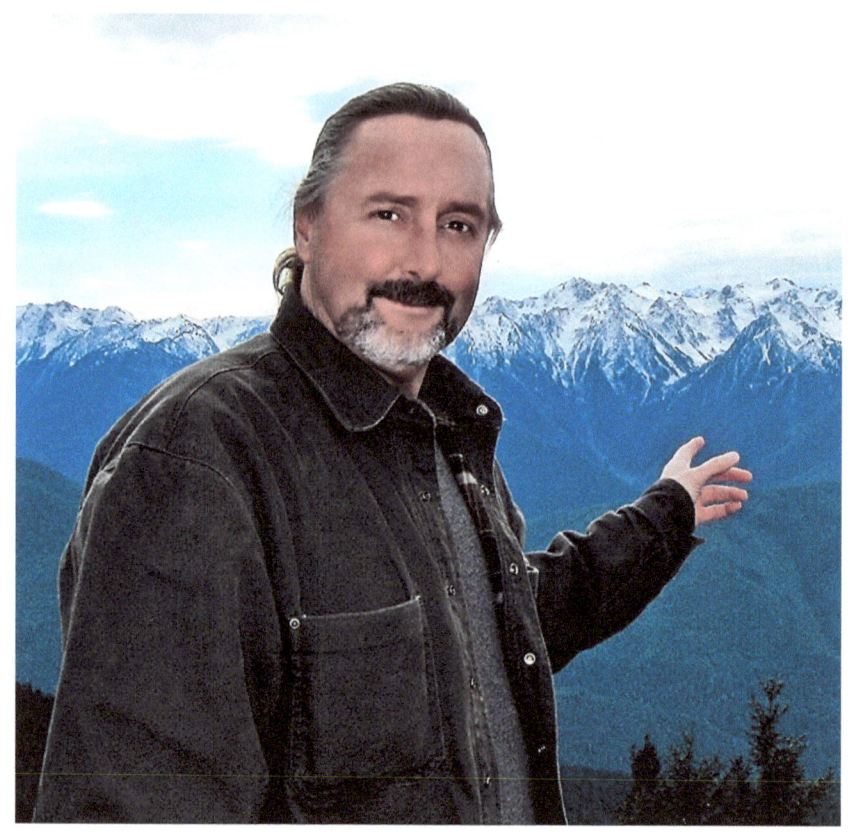

Joseph Fleming

Original Fine Art Photographs

Decades of being around accomplished talent producing absolutely phenomenal quality work has taught that we are capable of greatness. It is possible to meet our destiny and become it. Experiencing excellence done with such apparent ease and humble selfless gratification is the motivation for this photography. Most important was having the freedom

Being colorblind gives an advantage when composing black & white… less confusion.
This special collection selected from thousands of captures. All images were framed
in the camera and presented without edits, genuine as seen through the lens.
RAW conversion applied by proprietary panchromatic process.

Limited edition prints available from original source files.

info@ BEACHNOISE.com

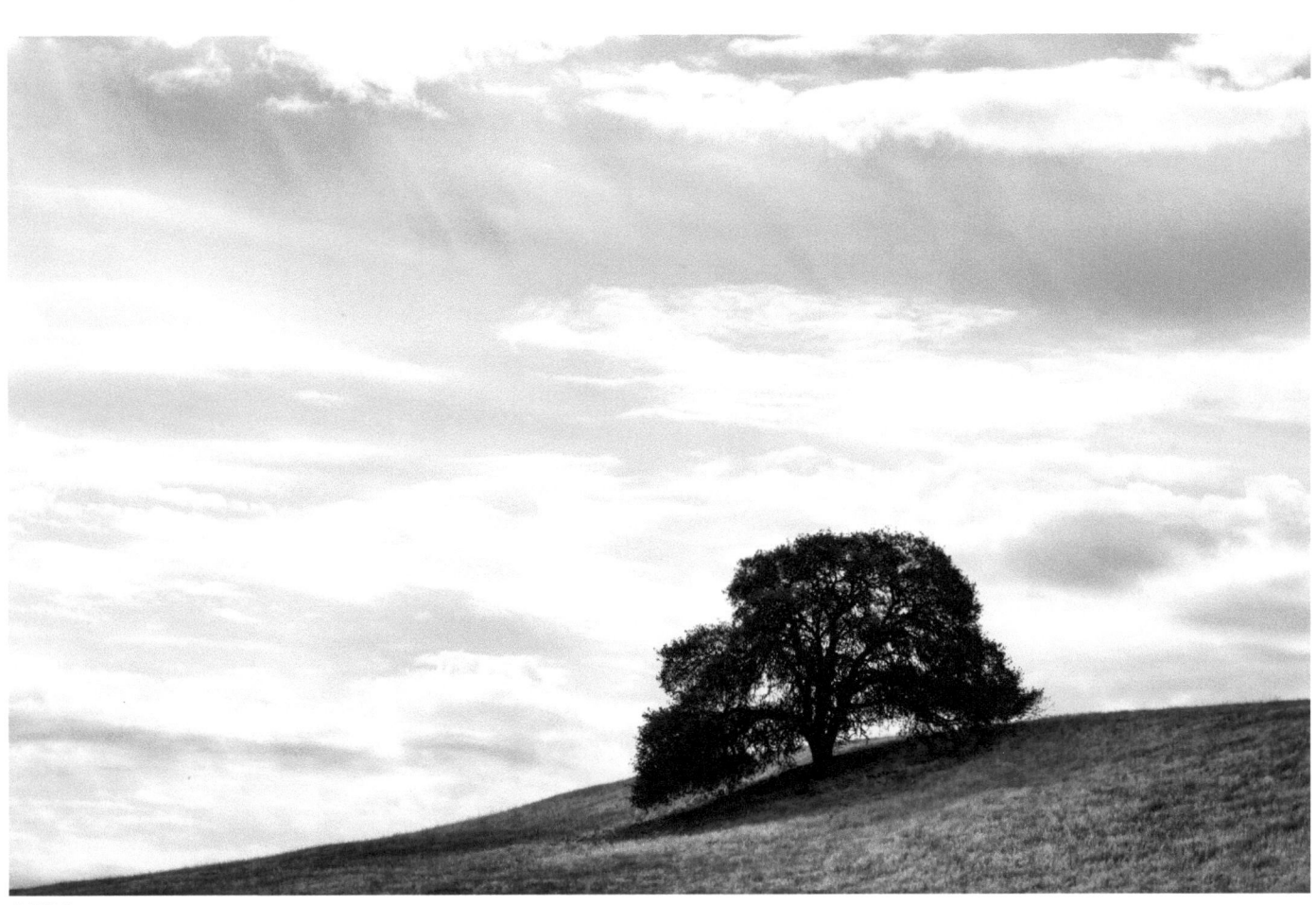

0531

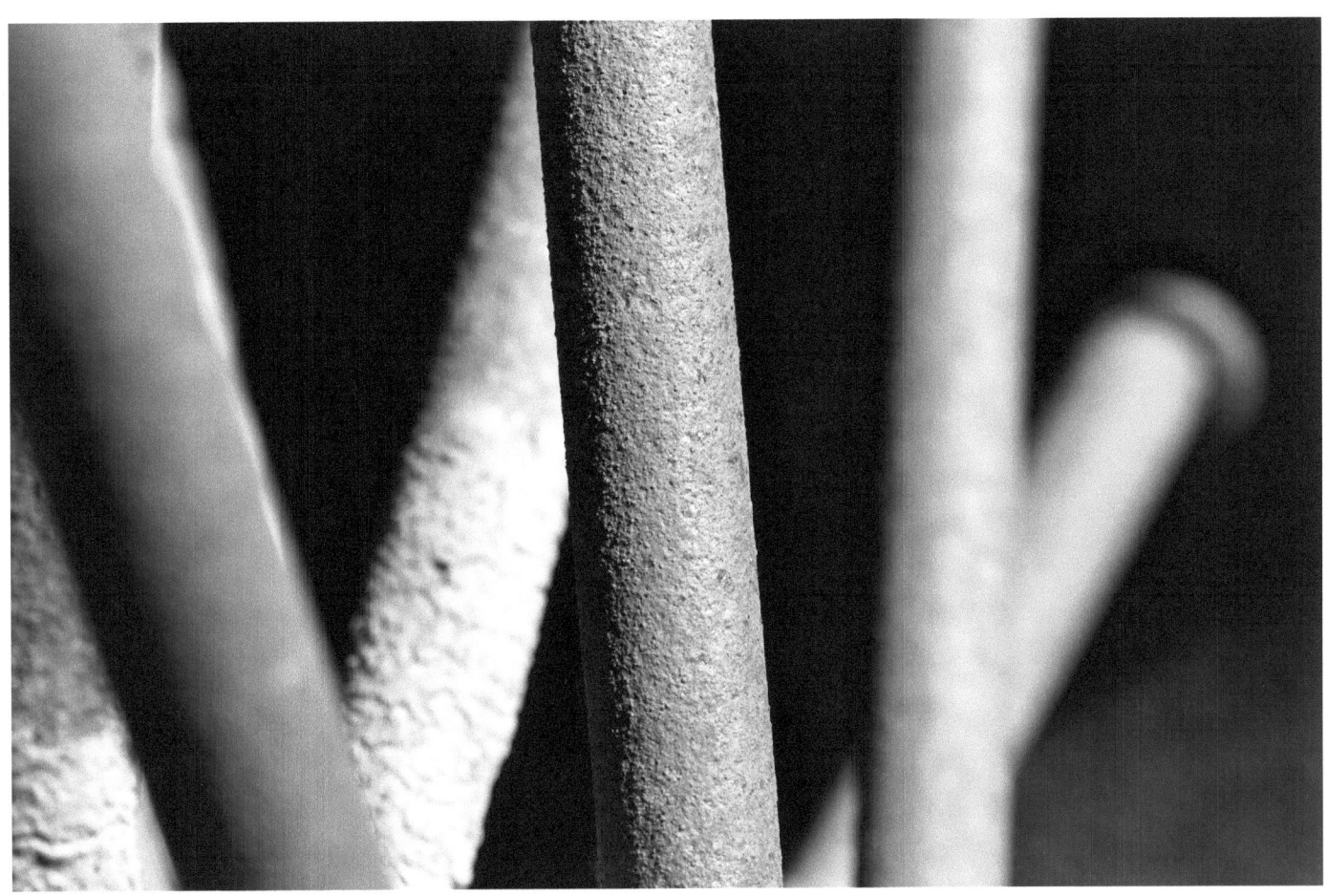

0780

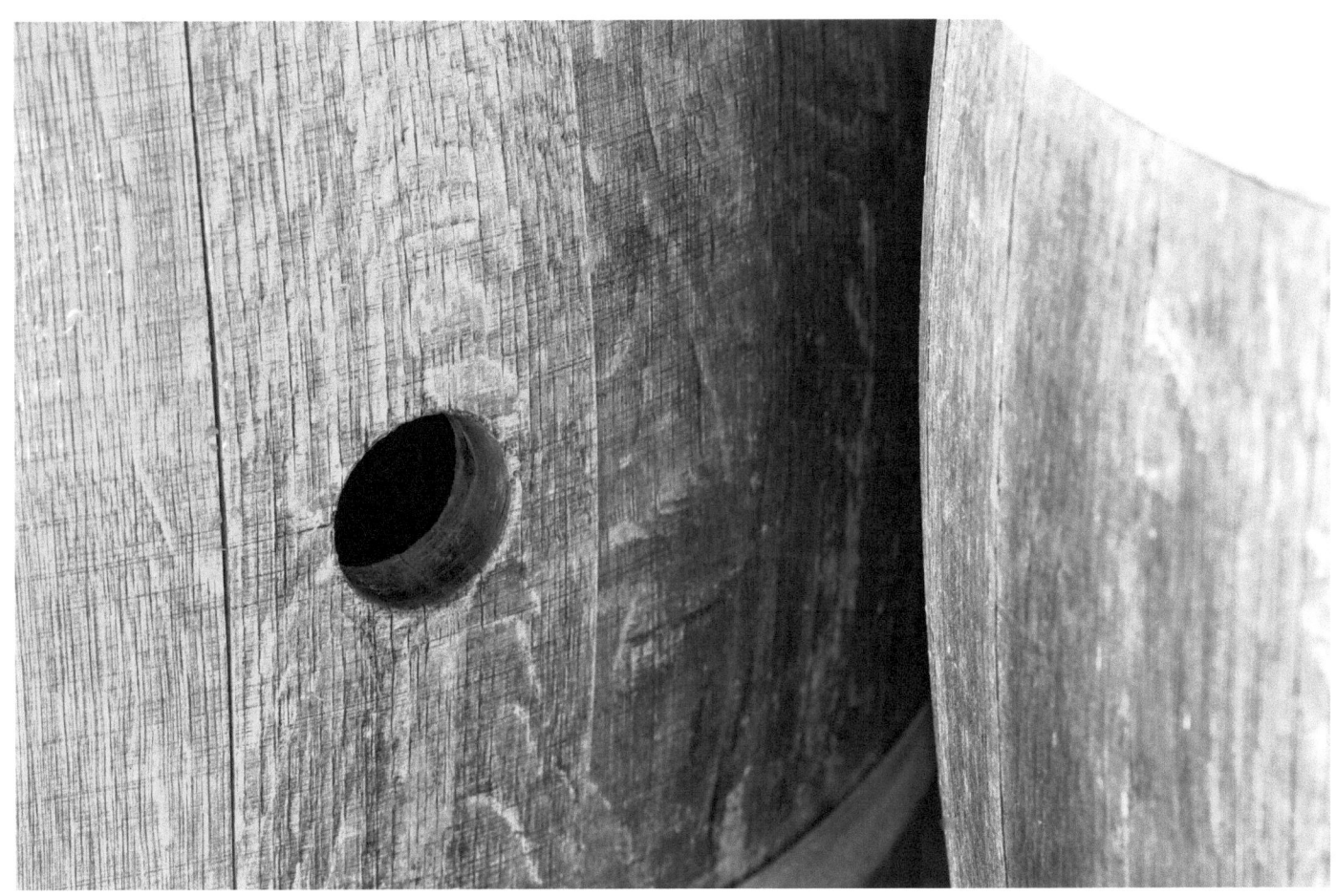

0826

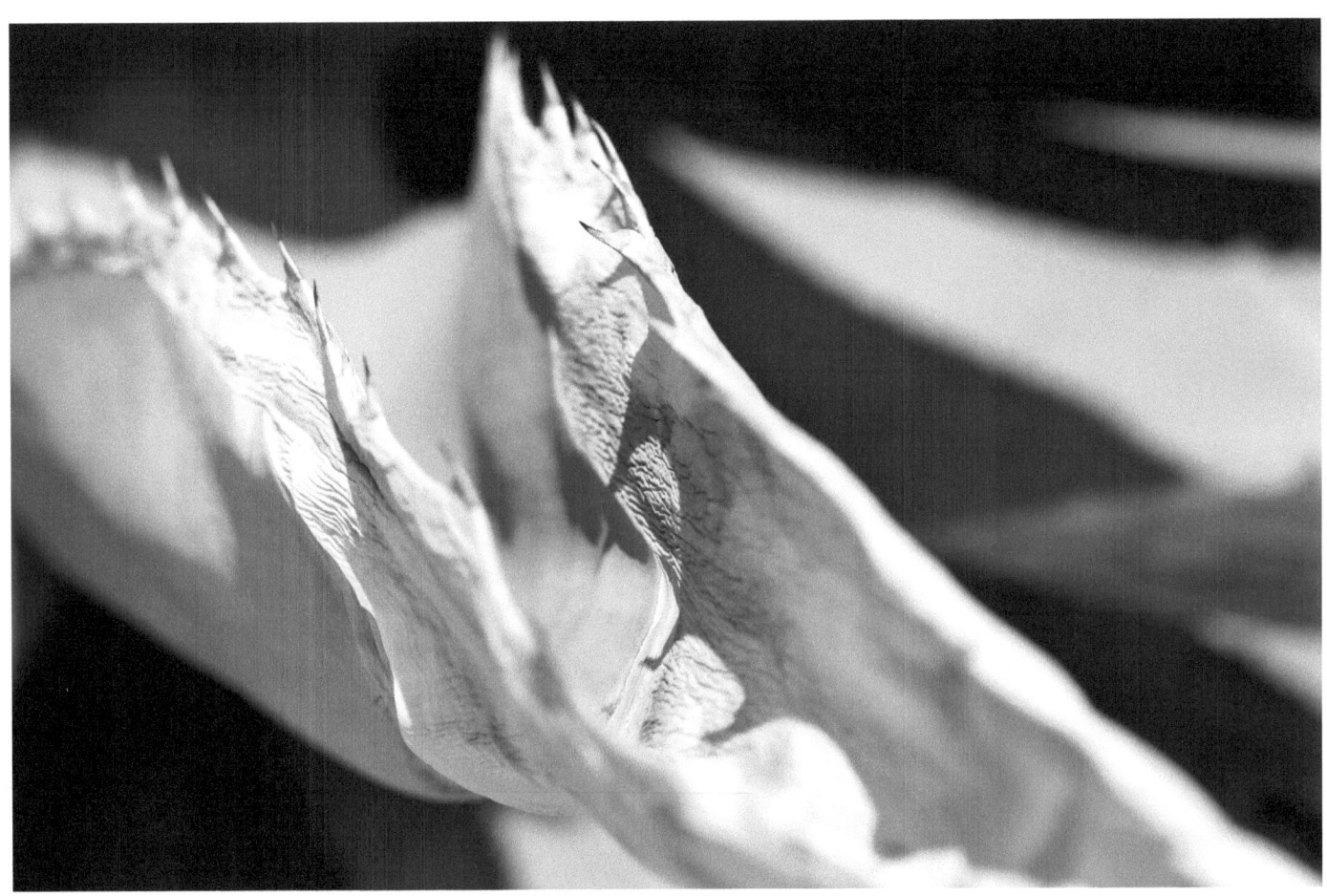

1581

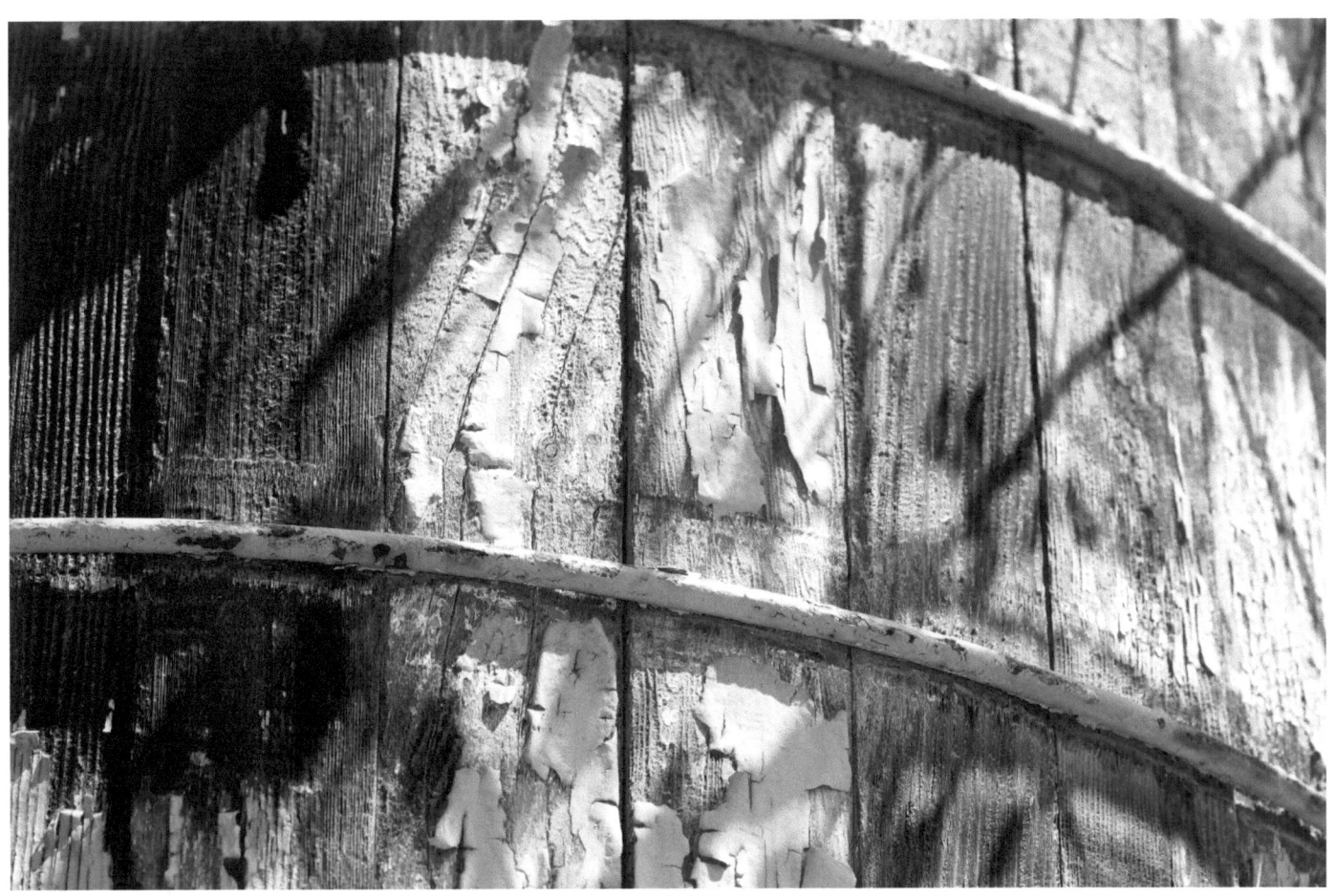

1608

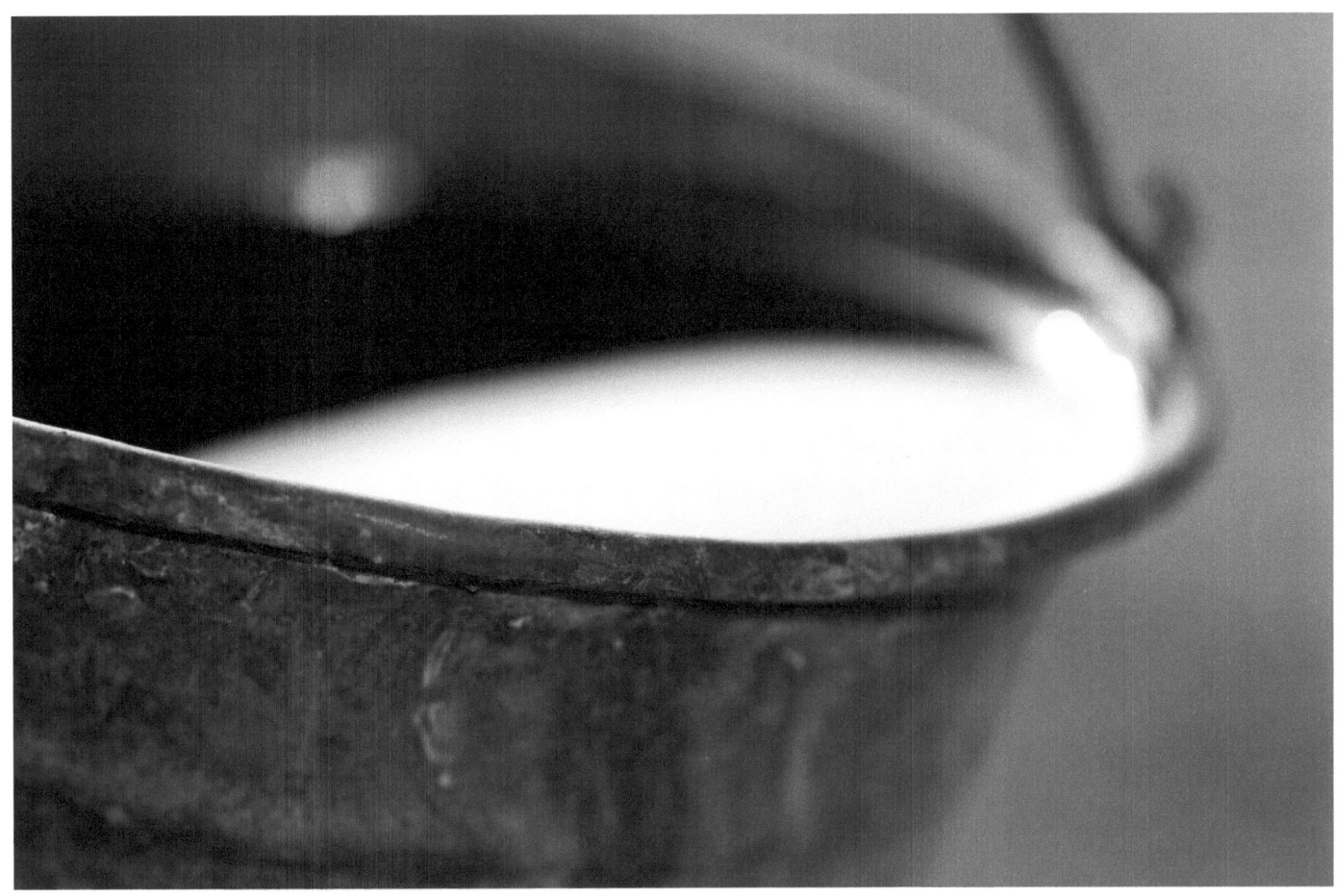

2180

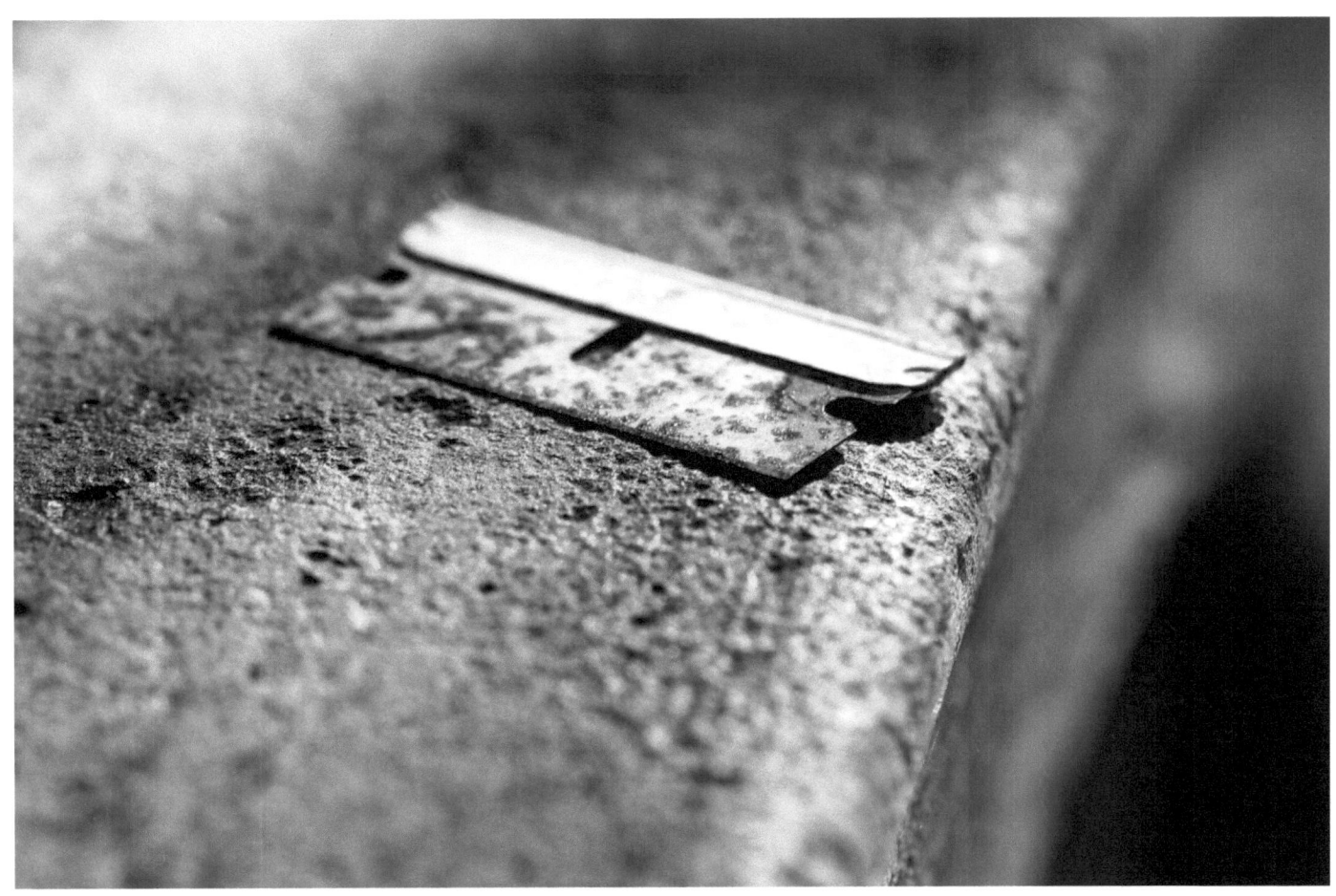

2467

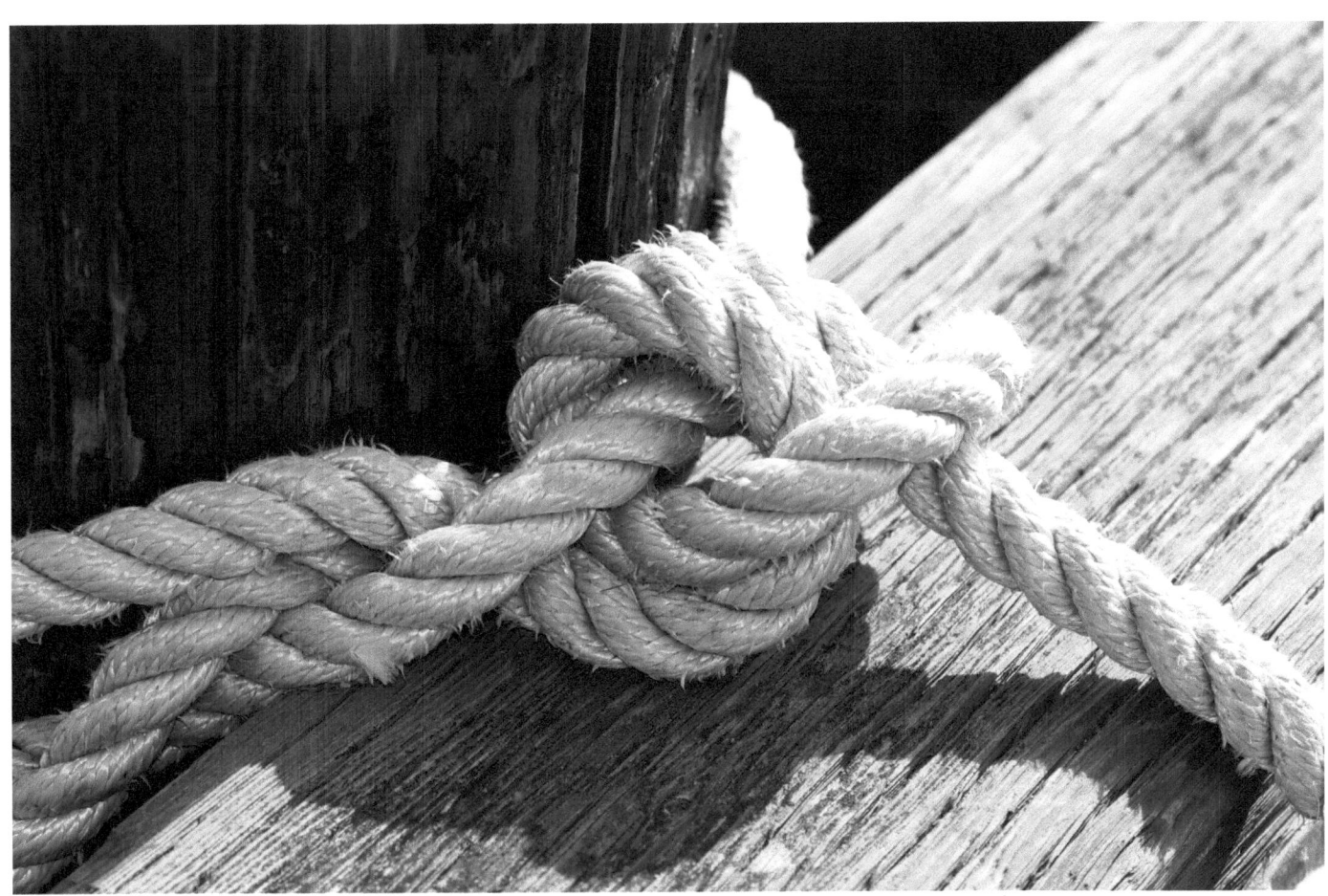

2631

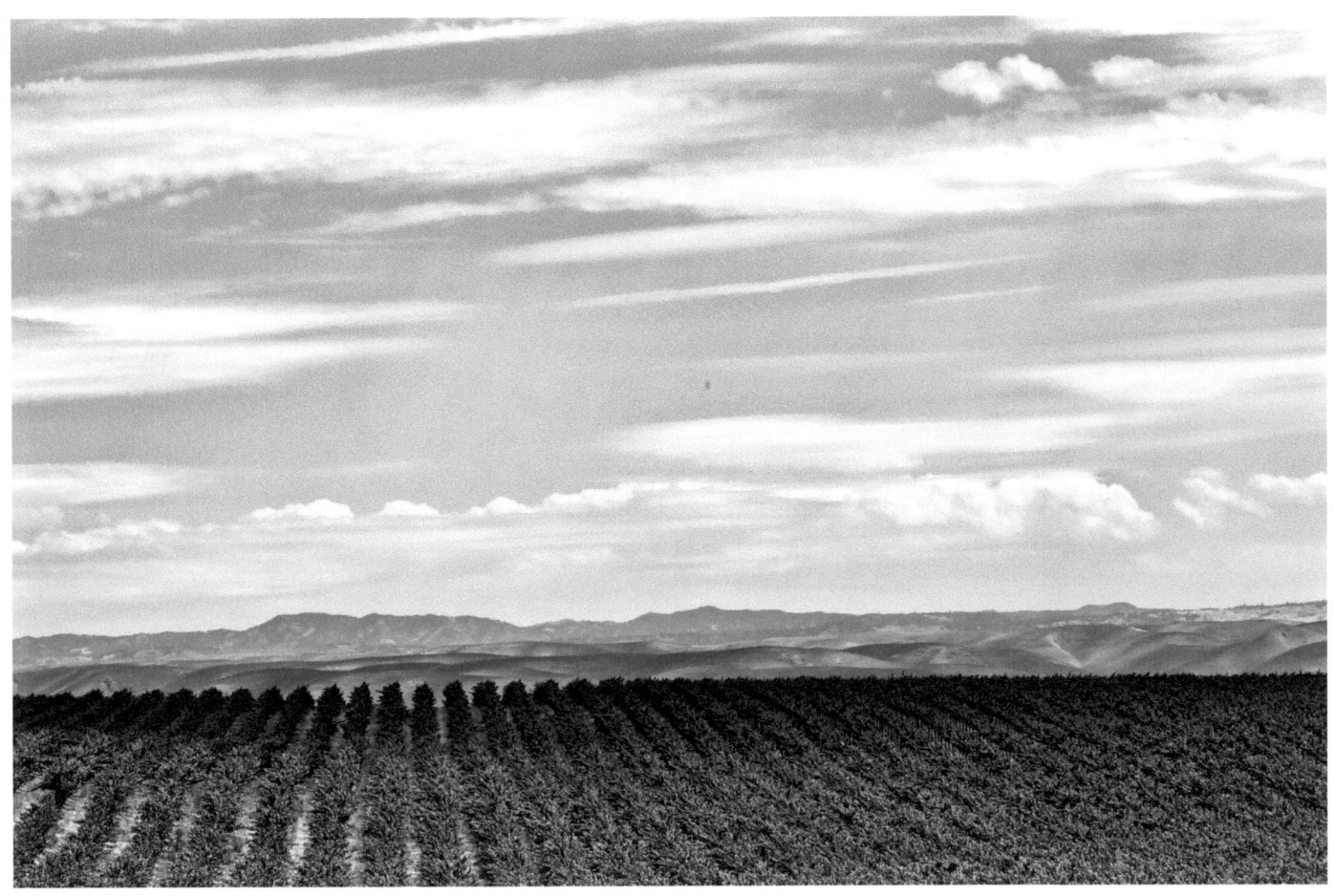

2929

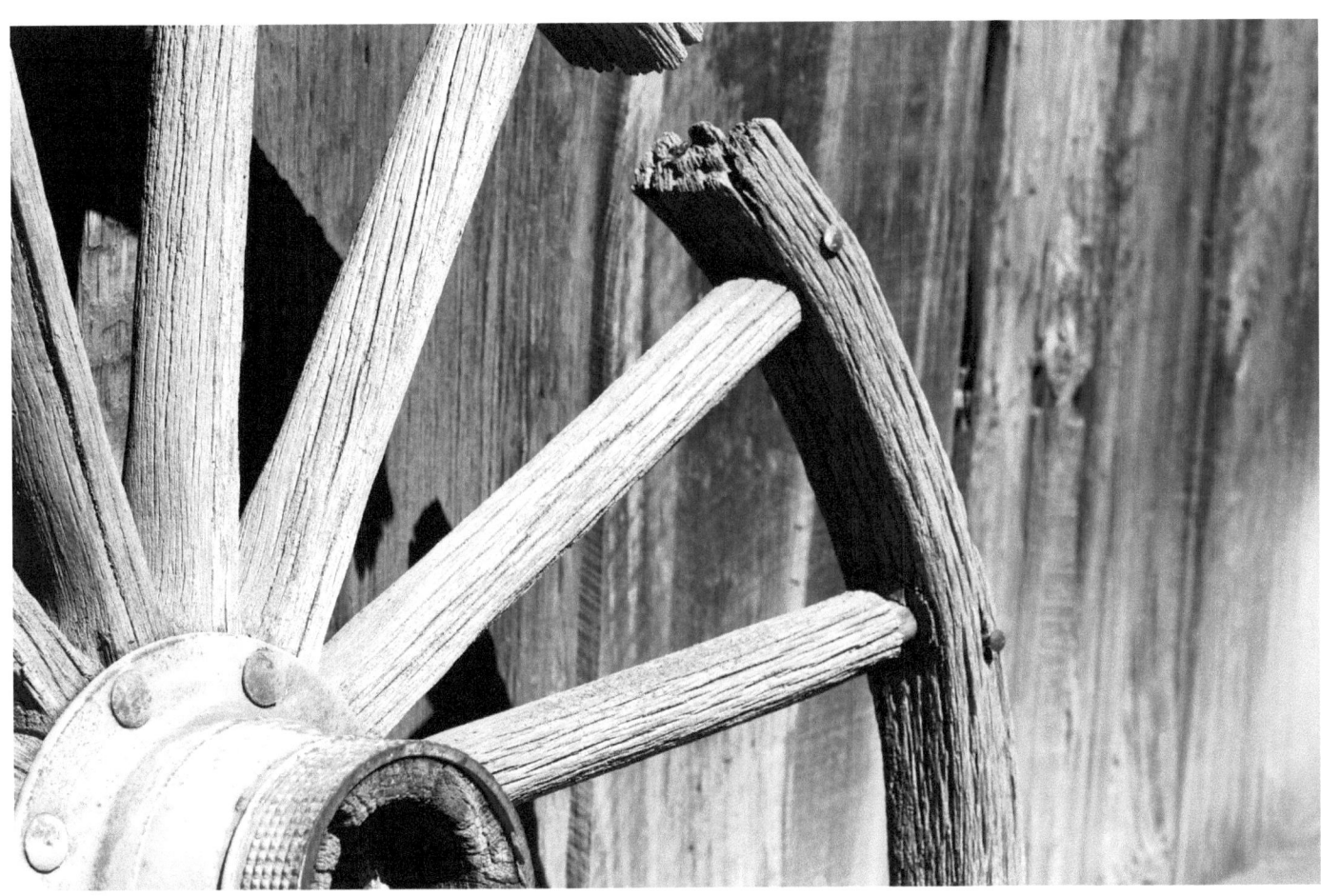

3147

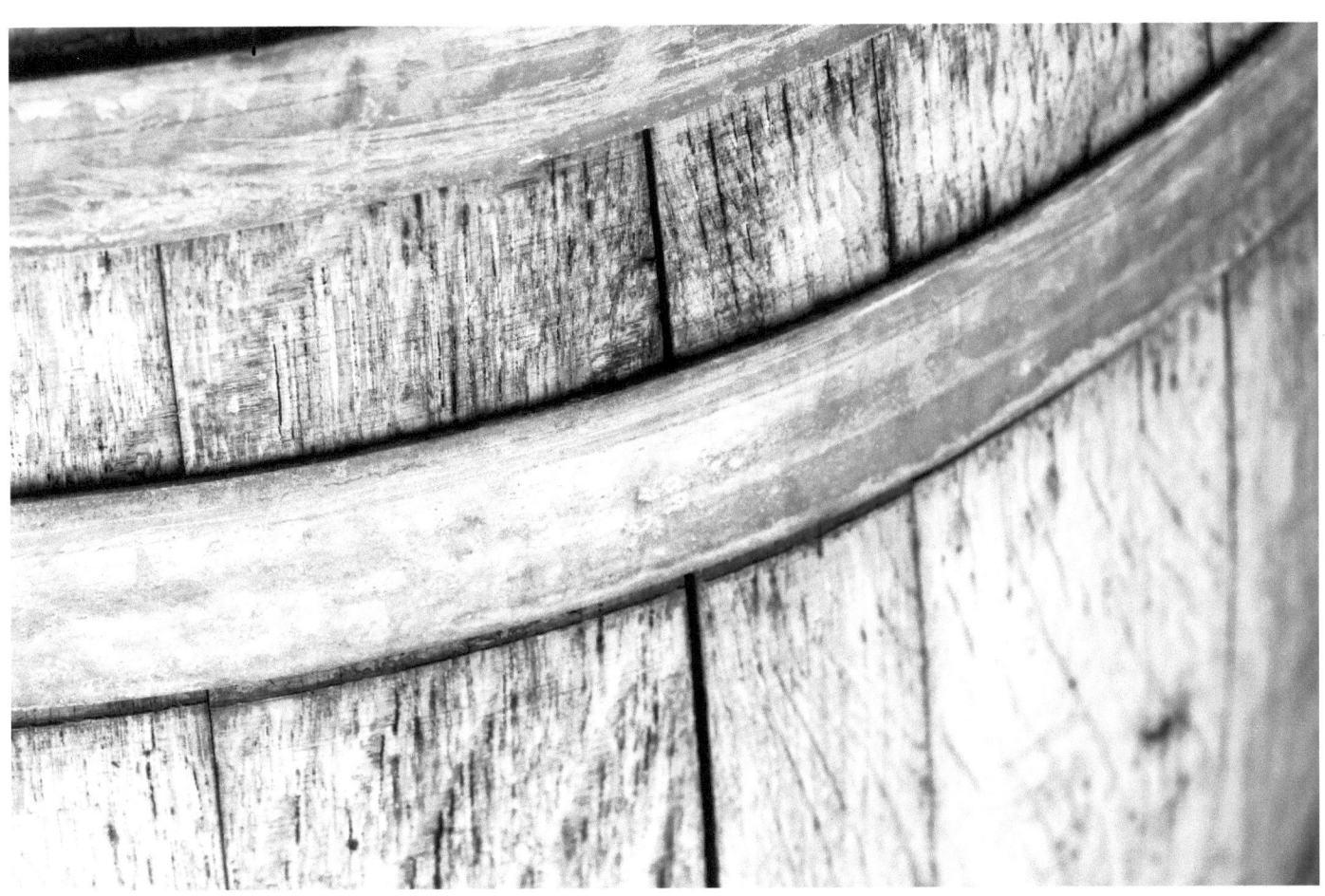

3151

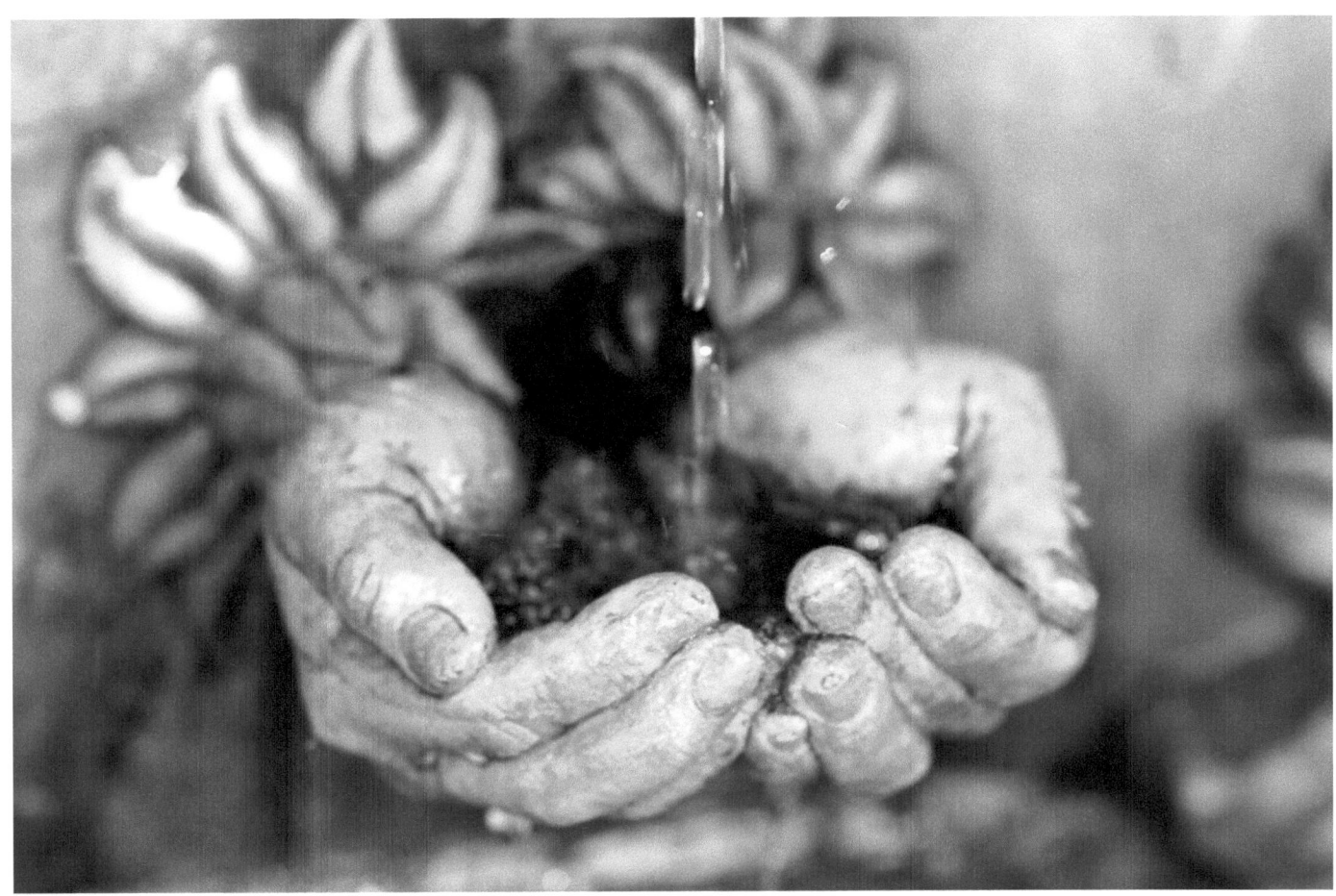

3720

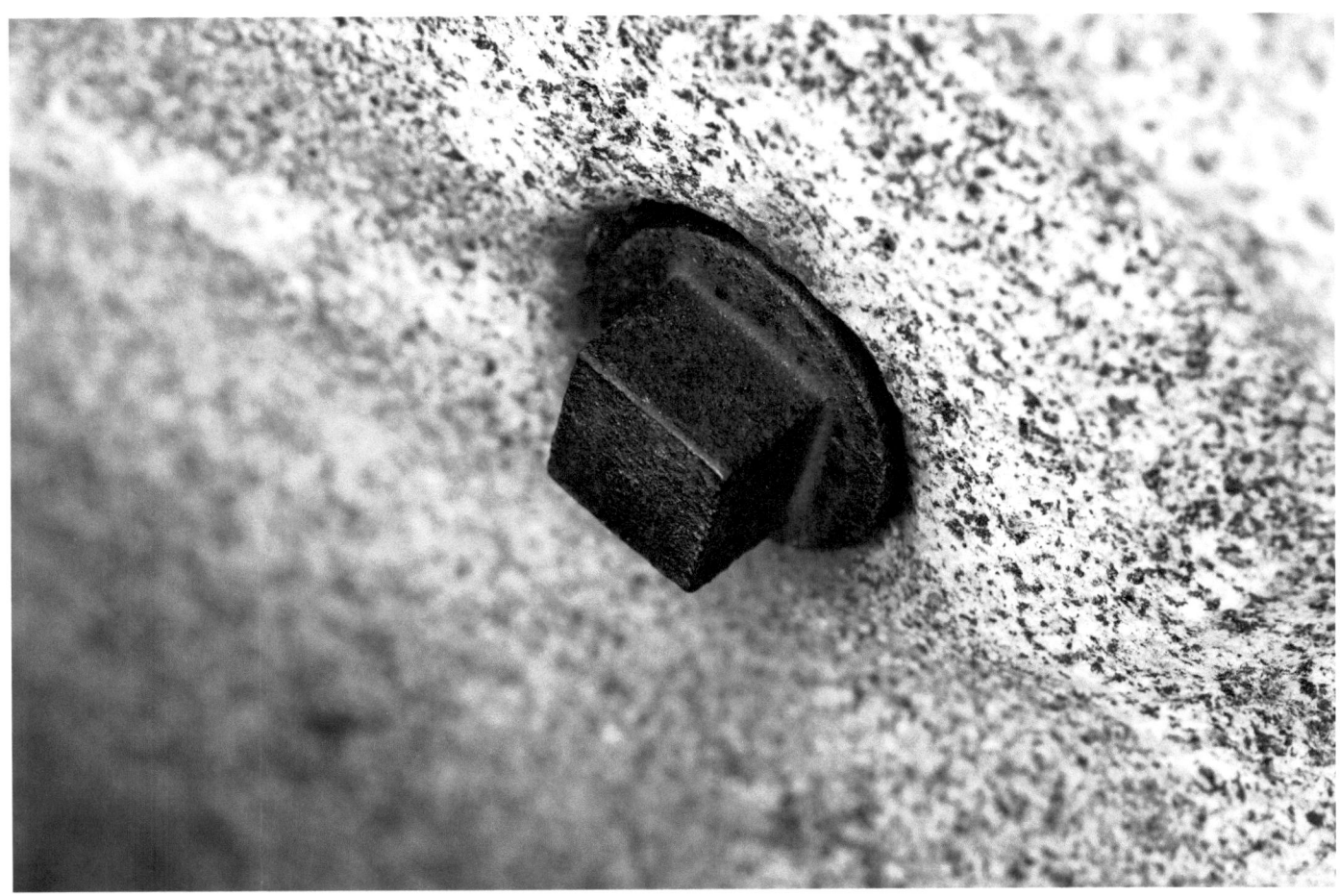

4035

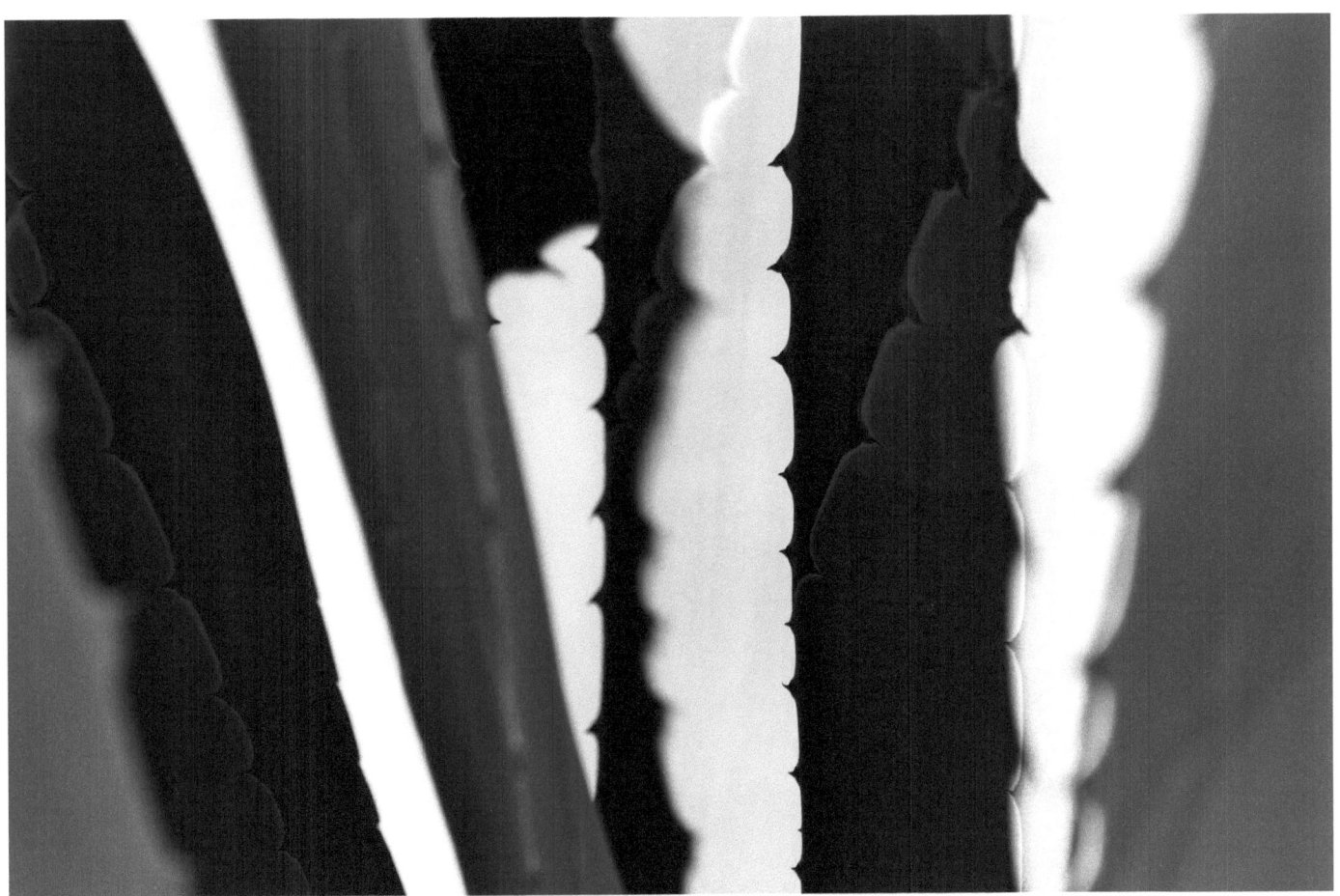

4099

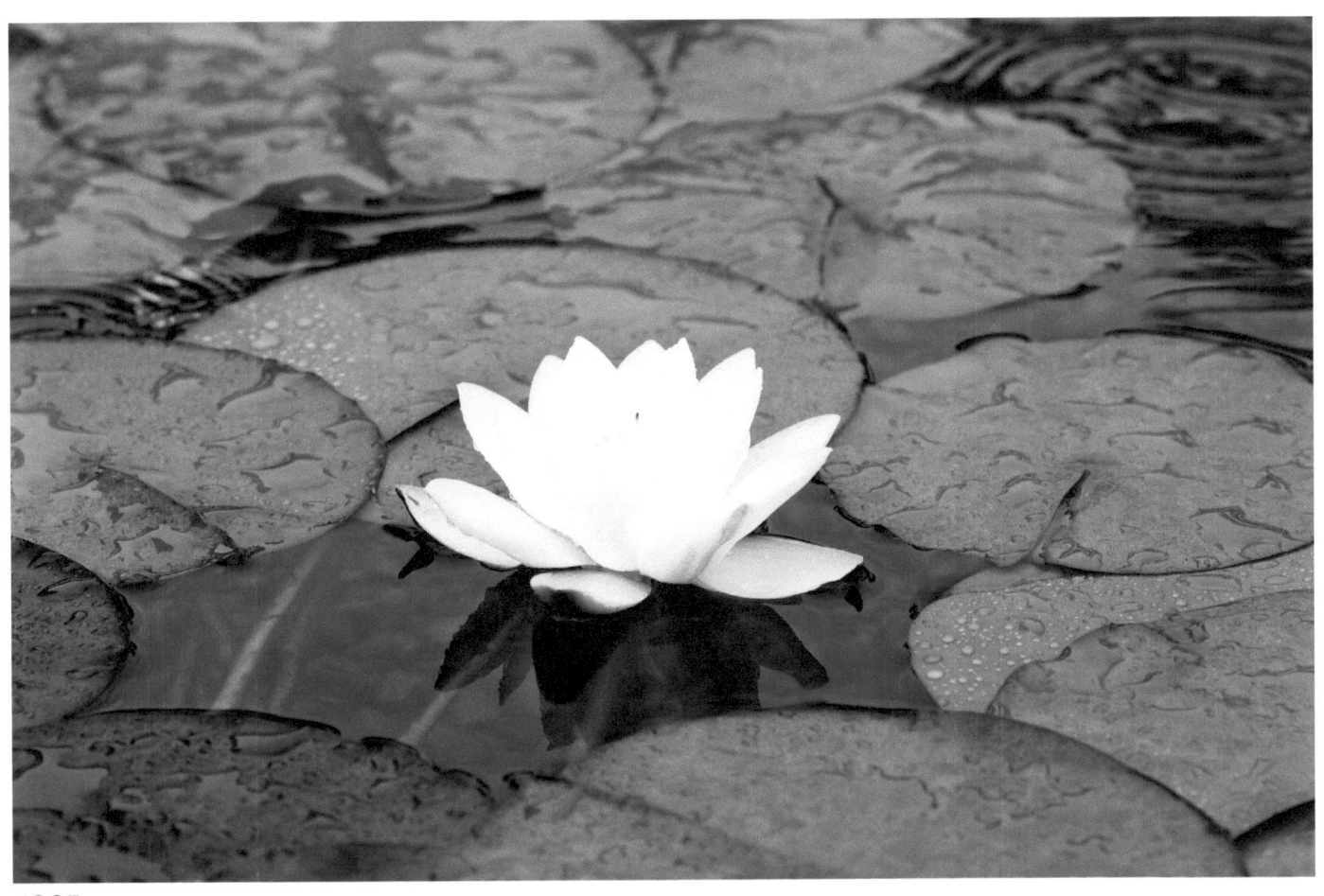

4265

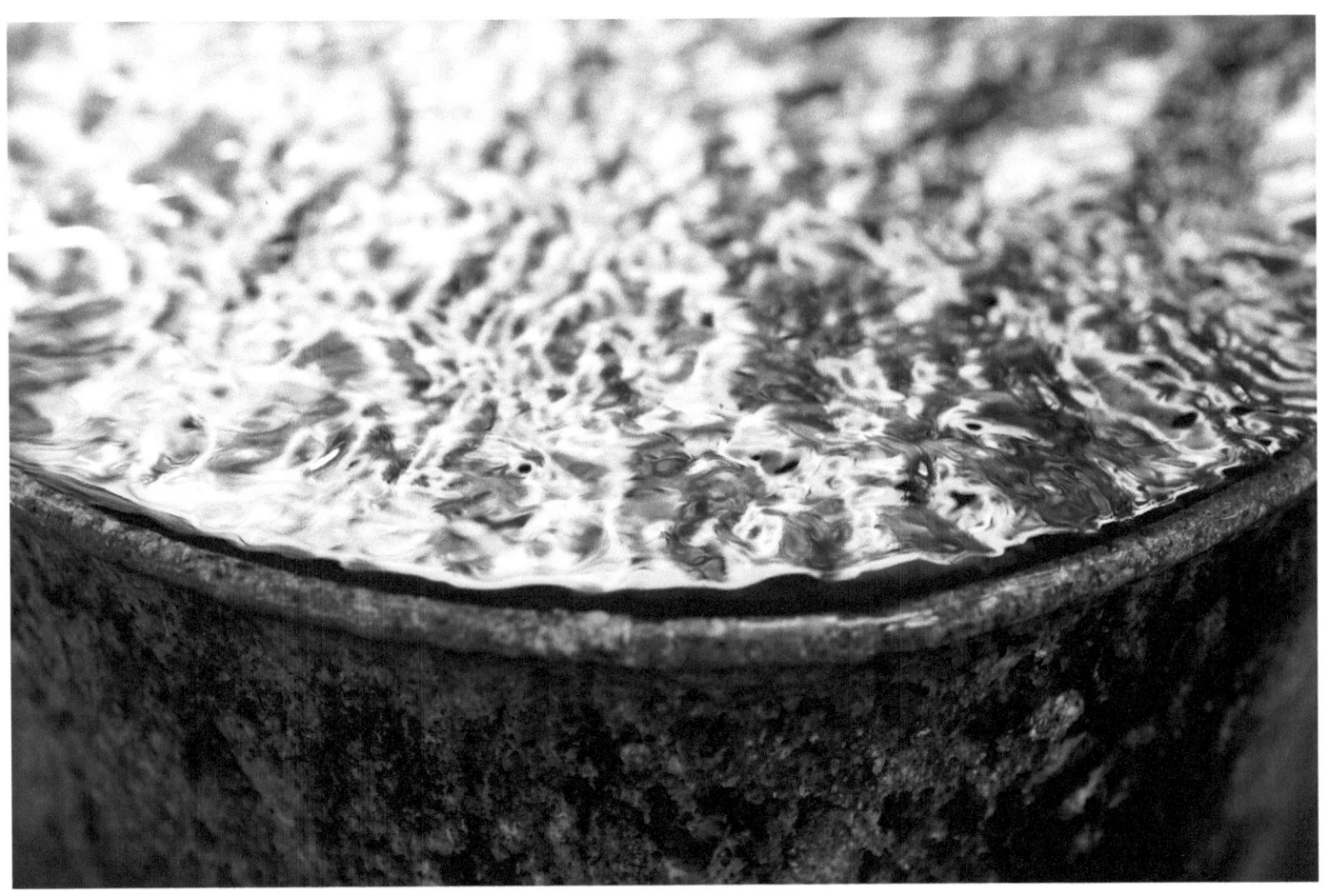

4533

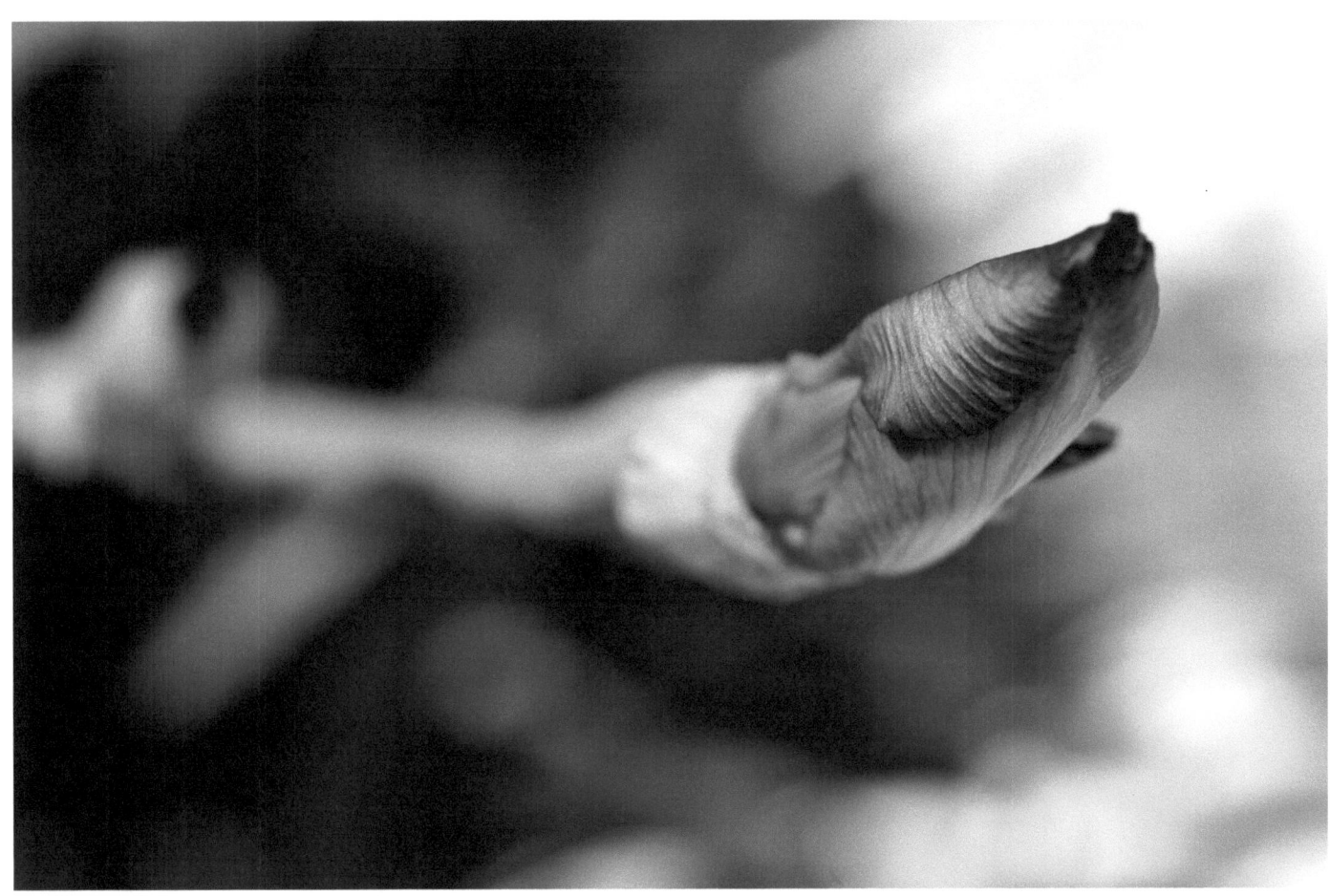

5492

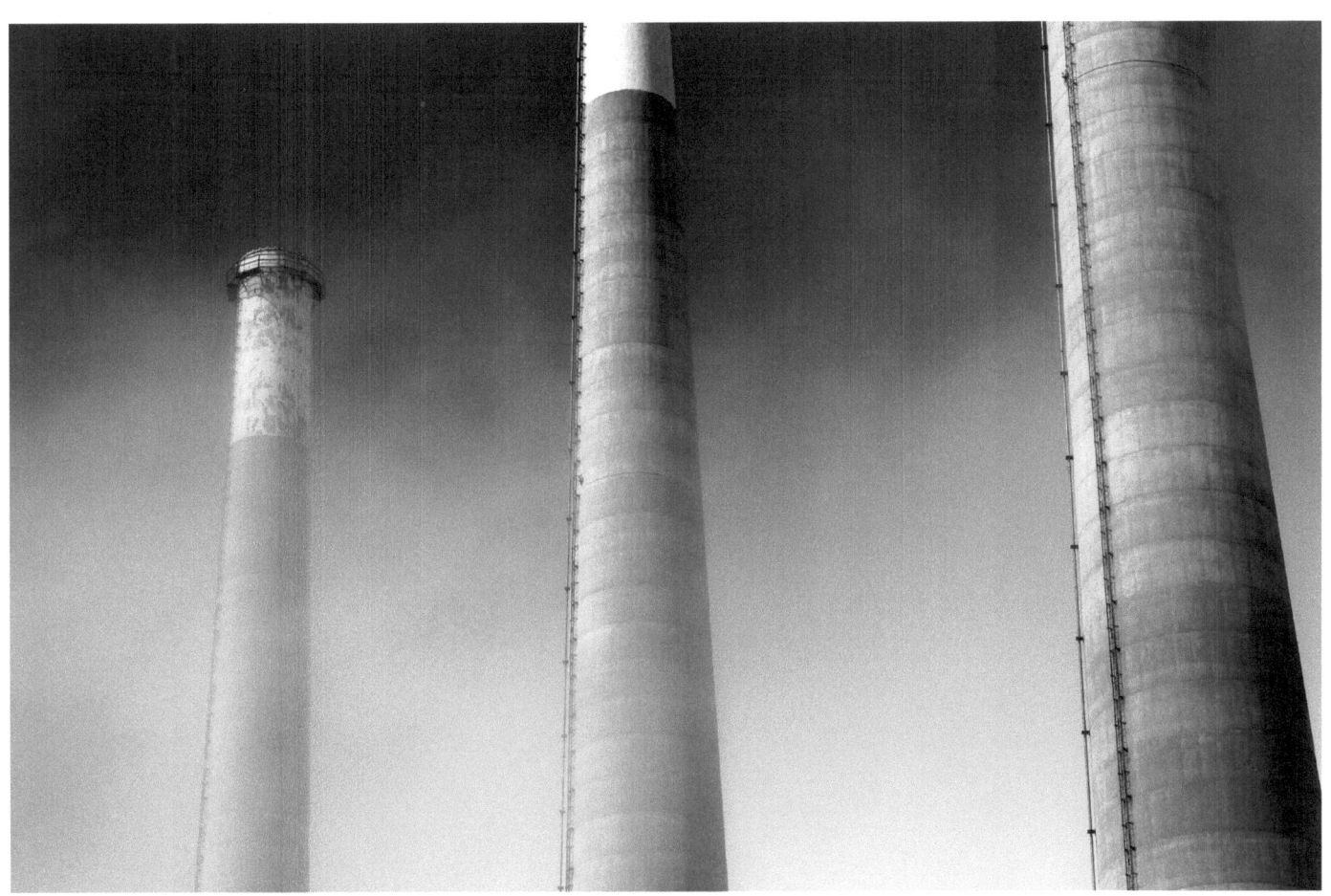

5541

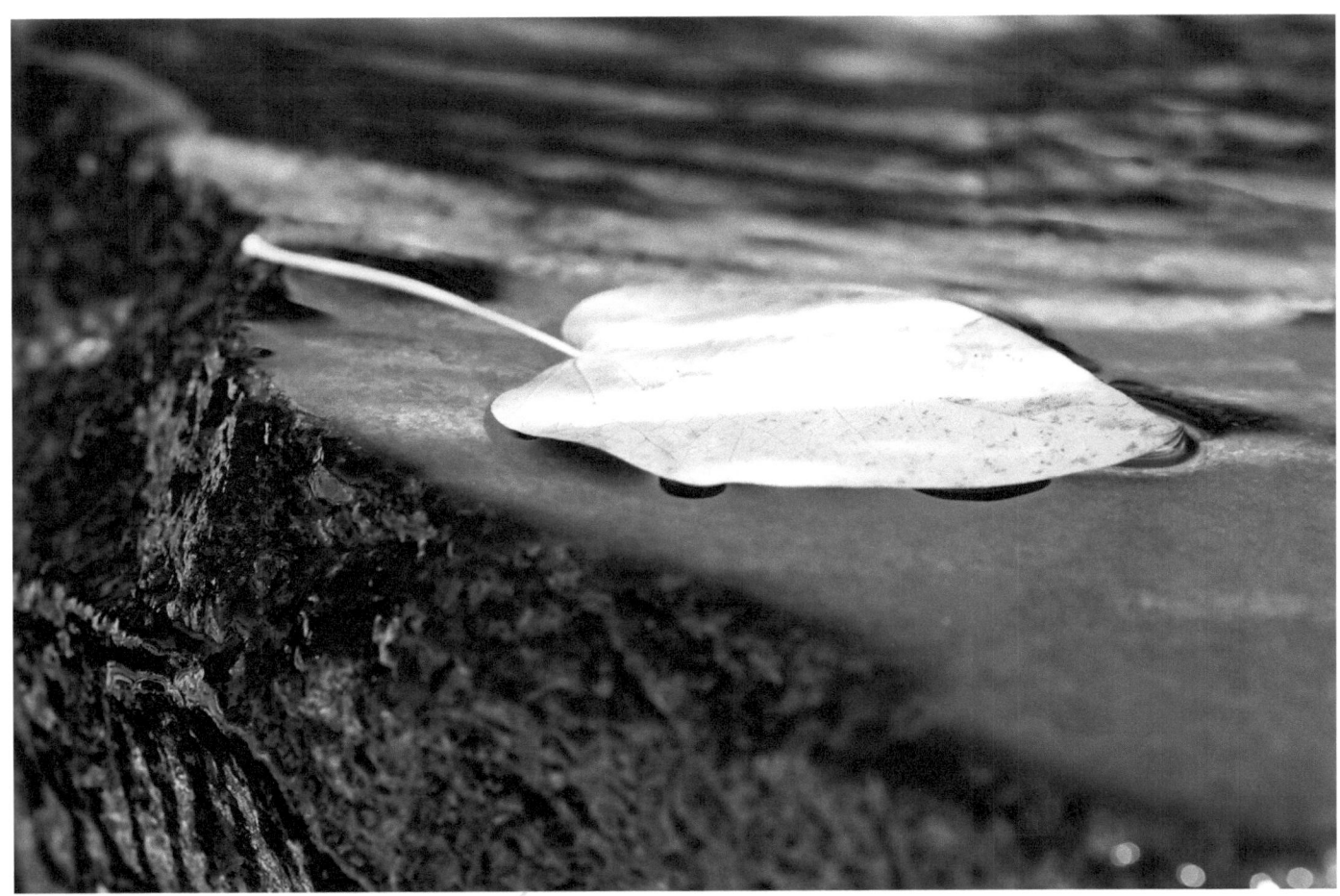

5750

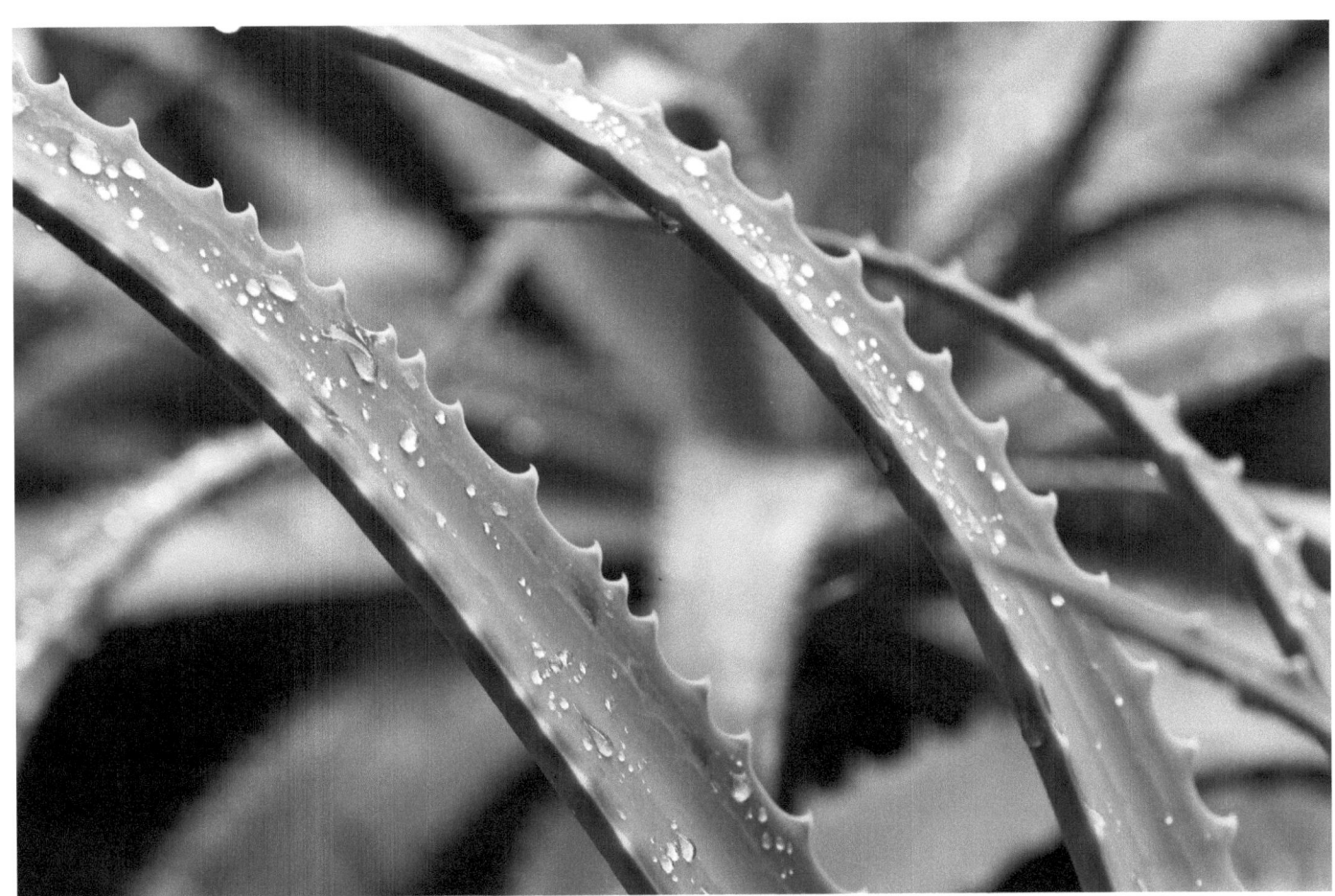

5784

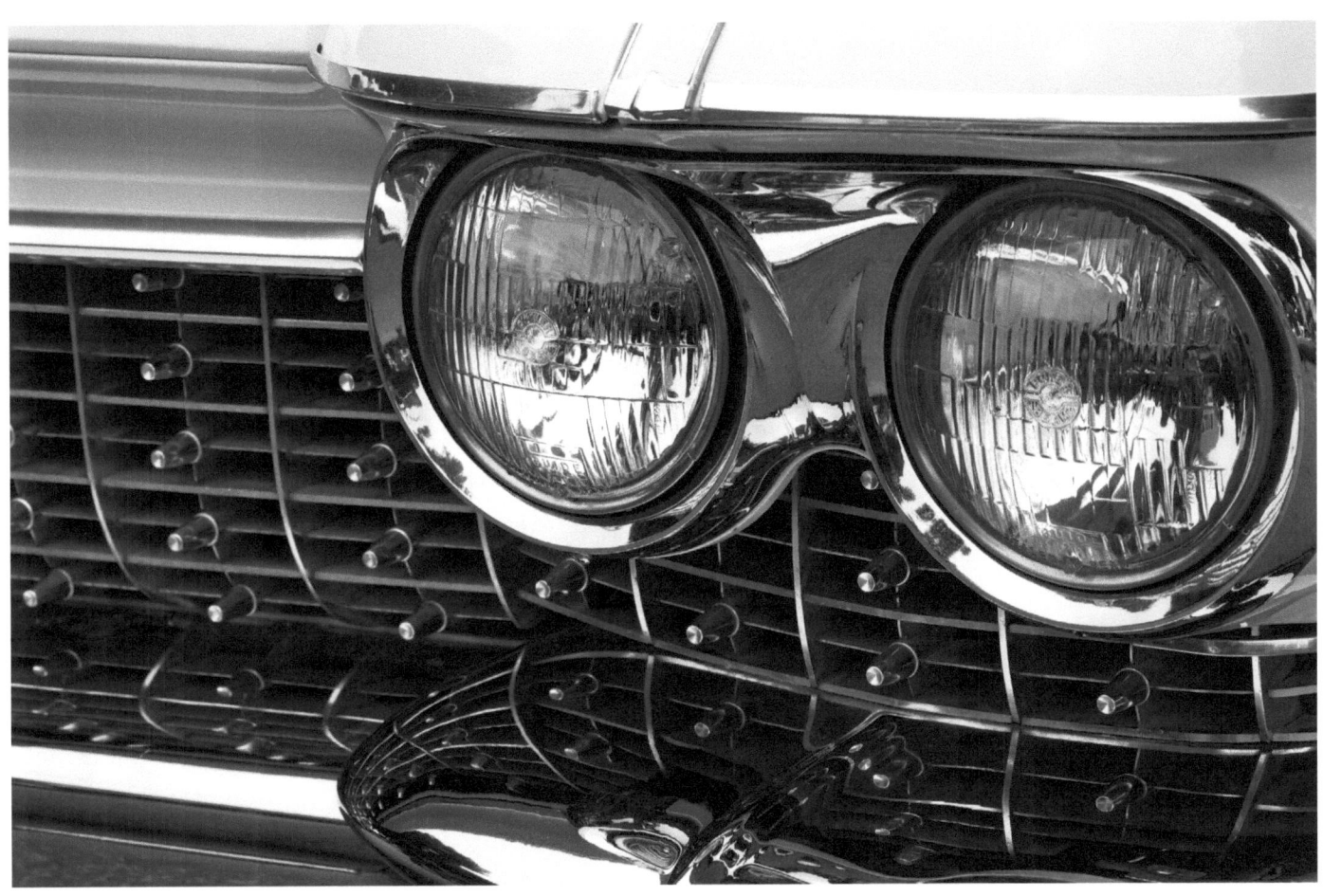

5844

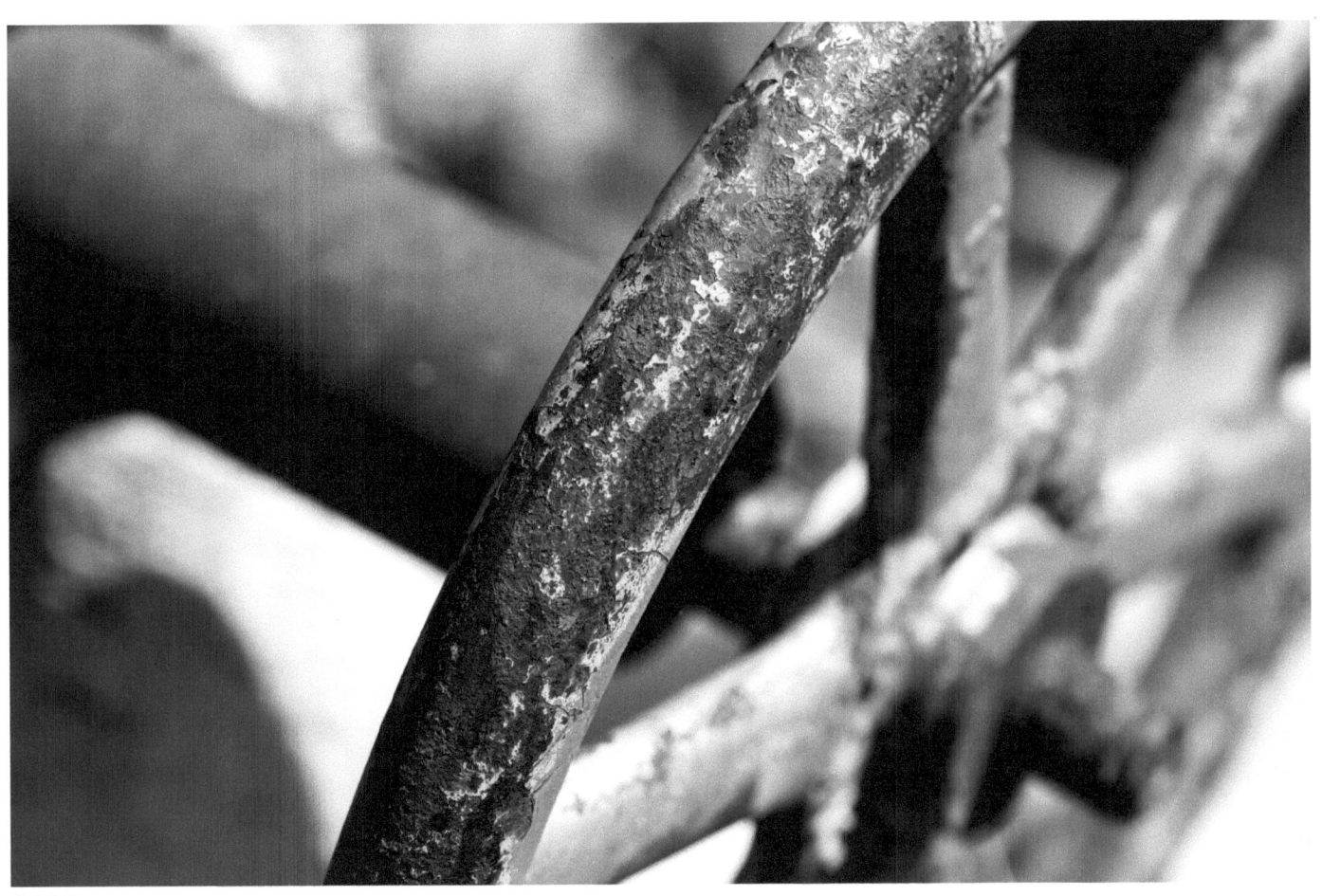

6095

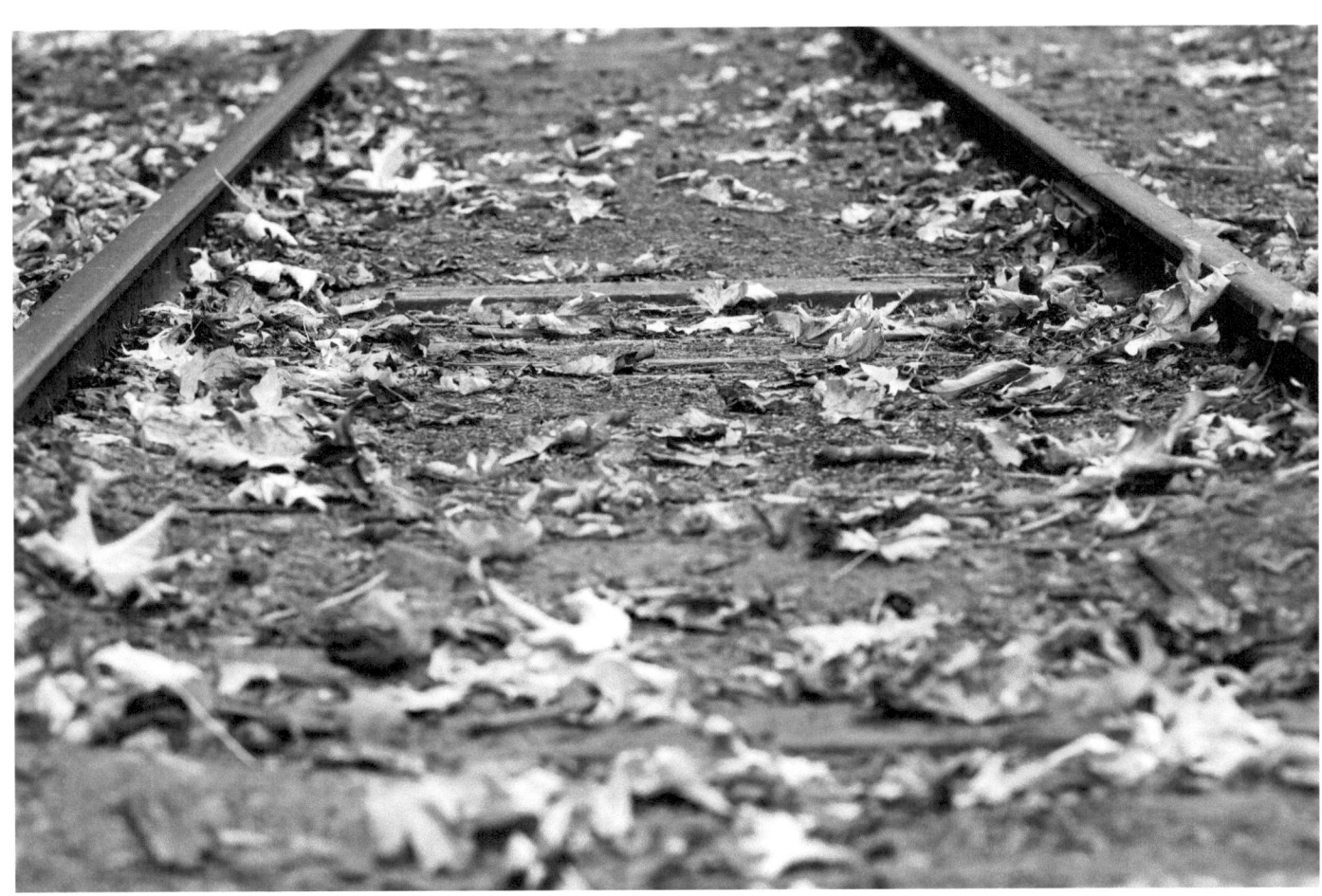

6176

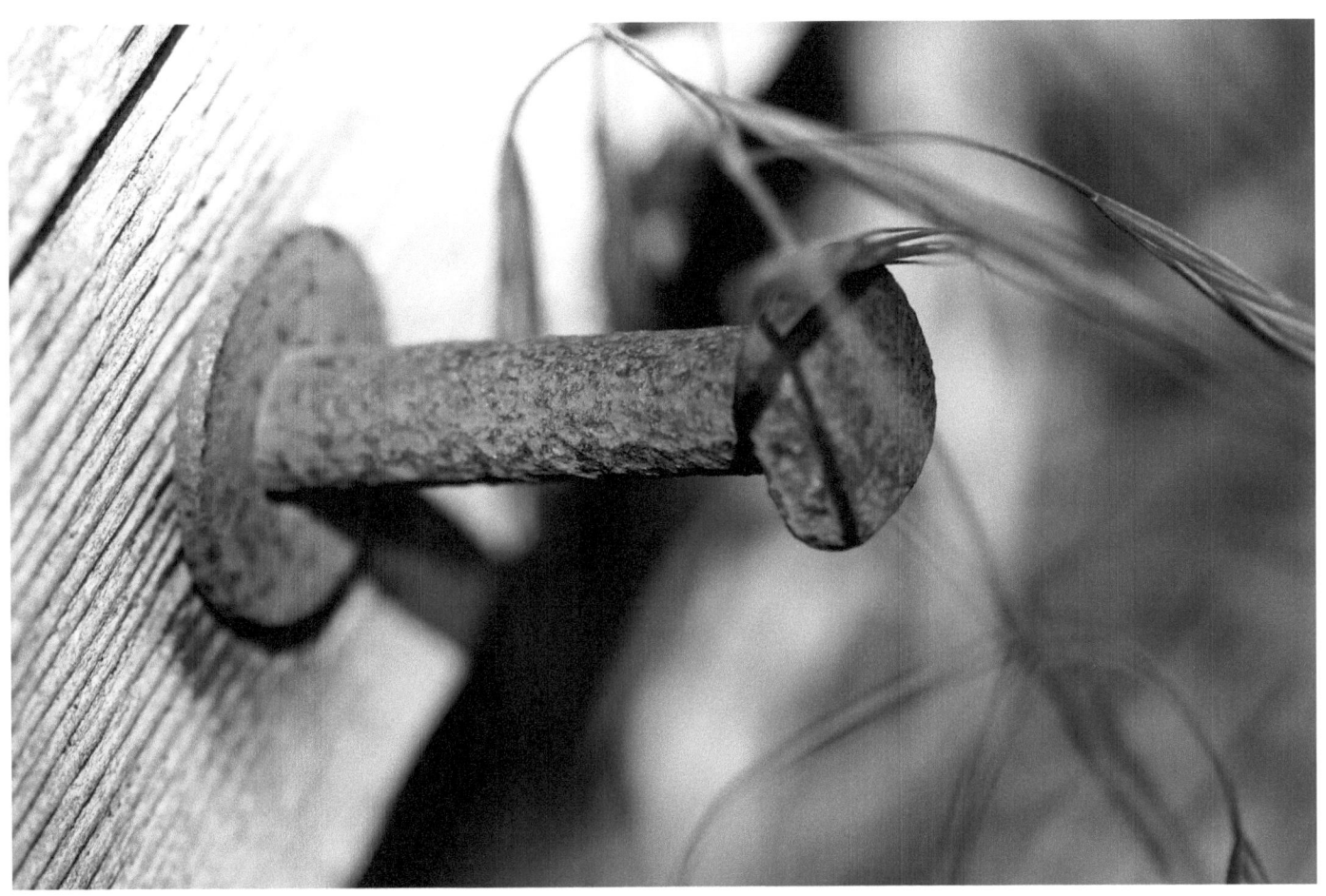

7182

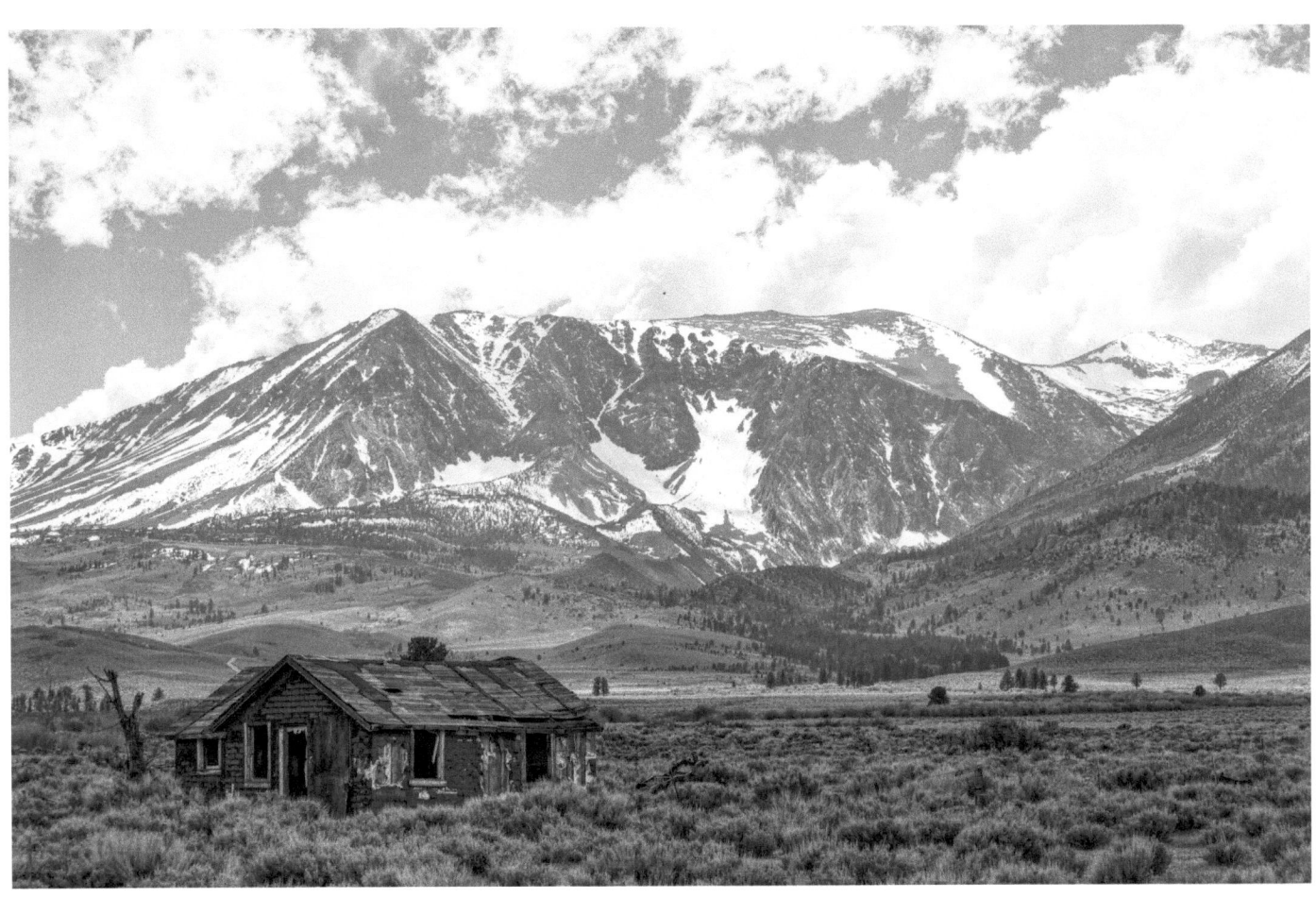

7339

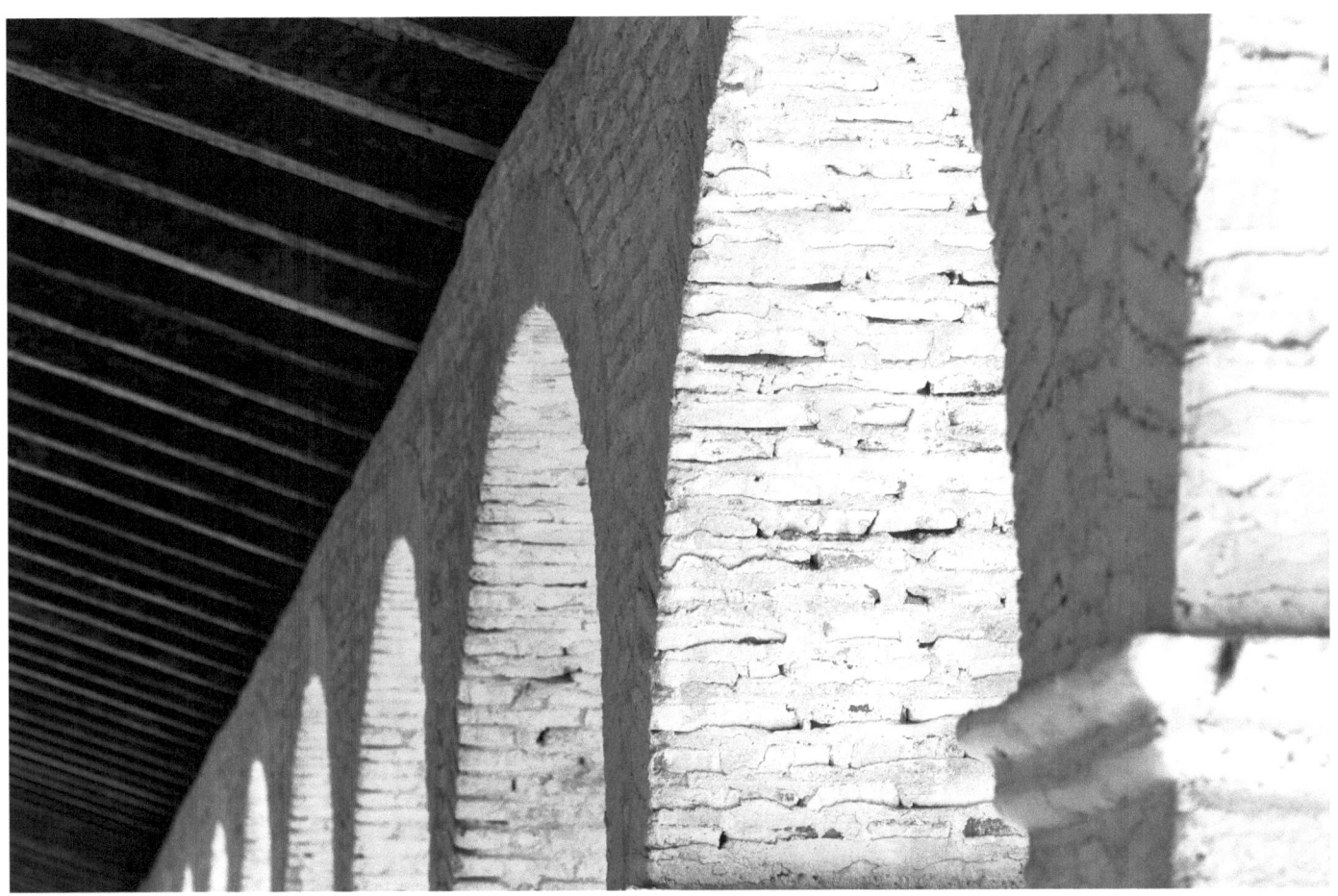

7656

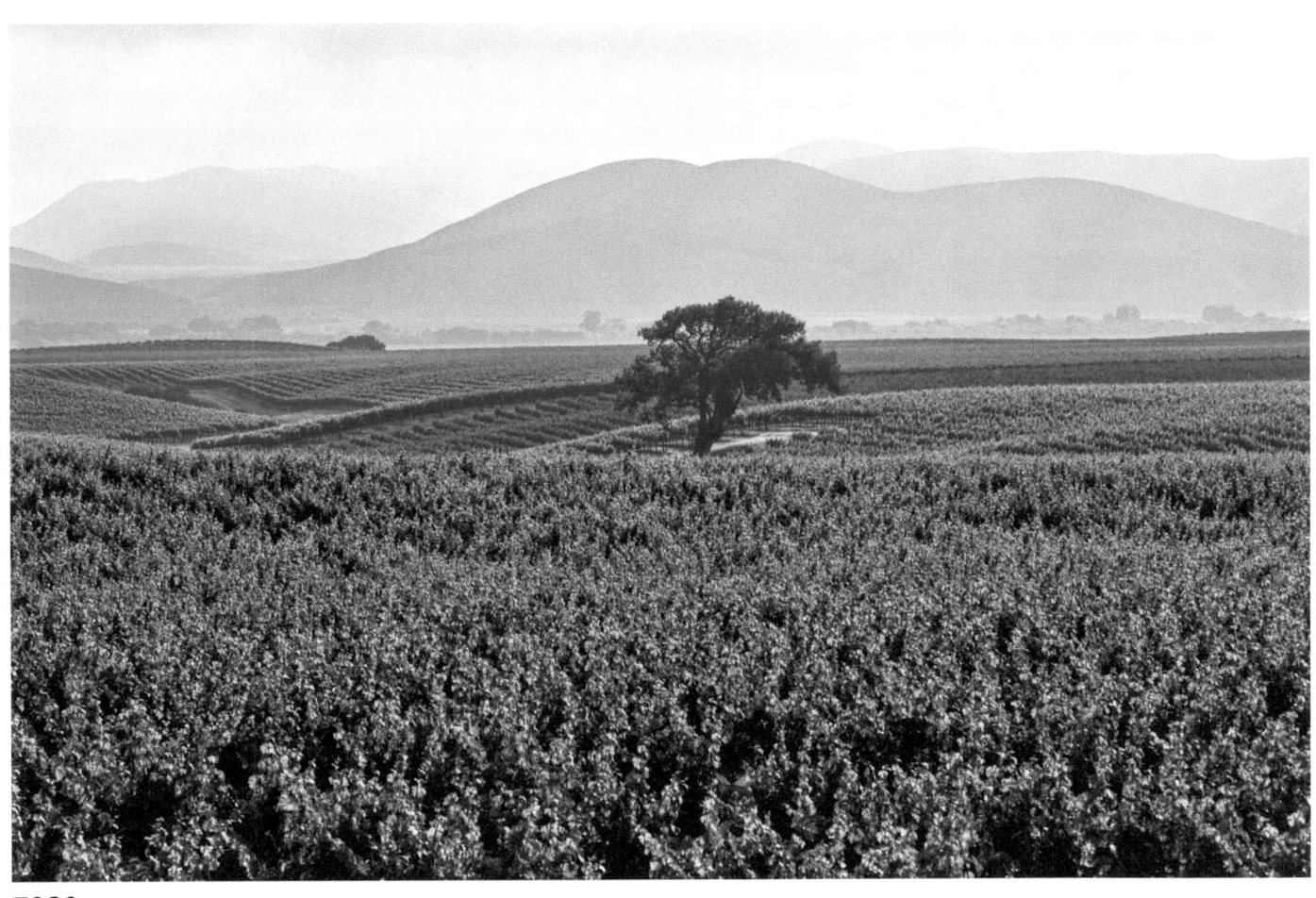

7939

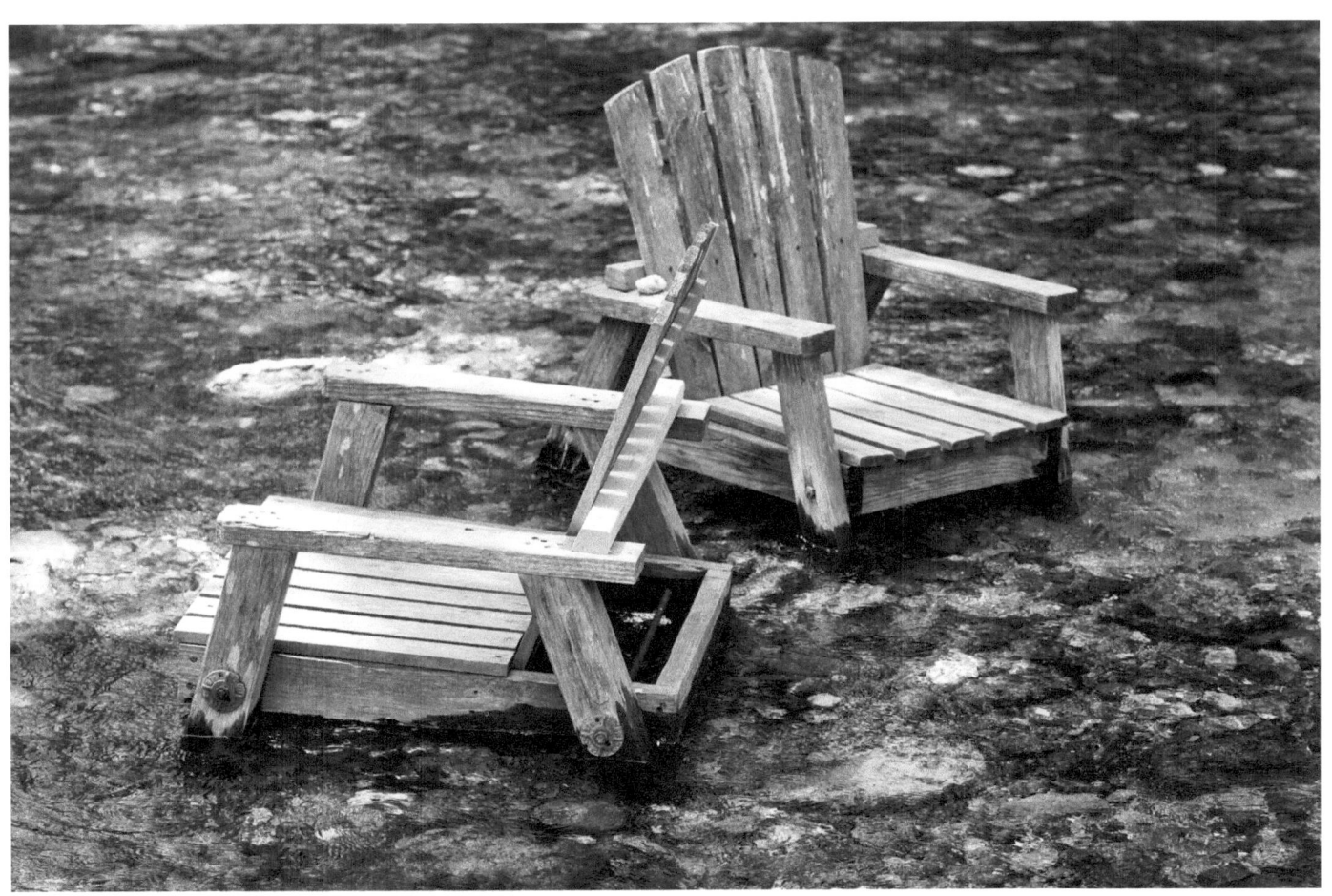

8173

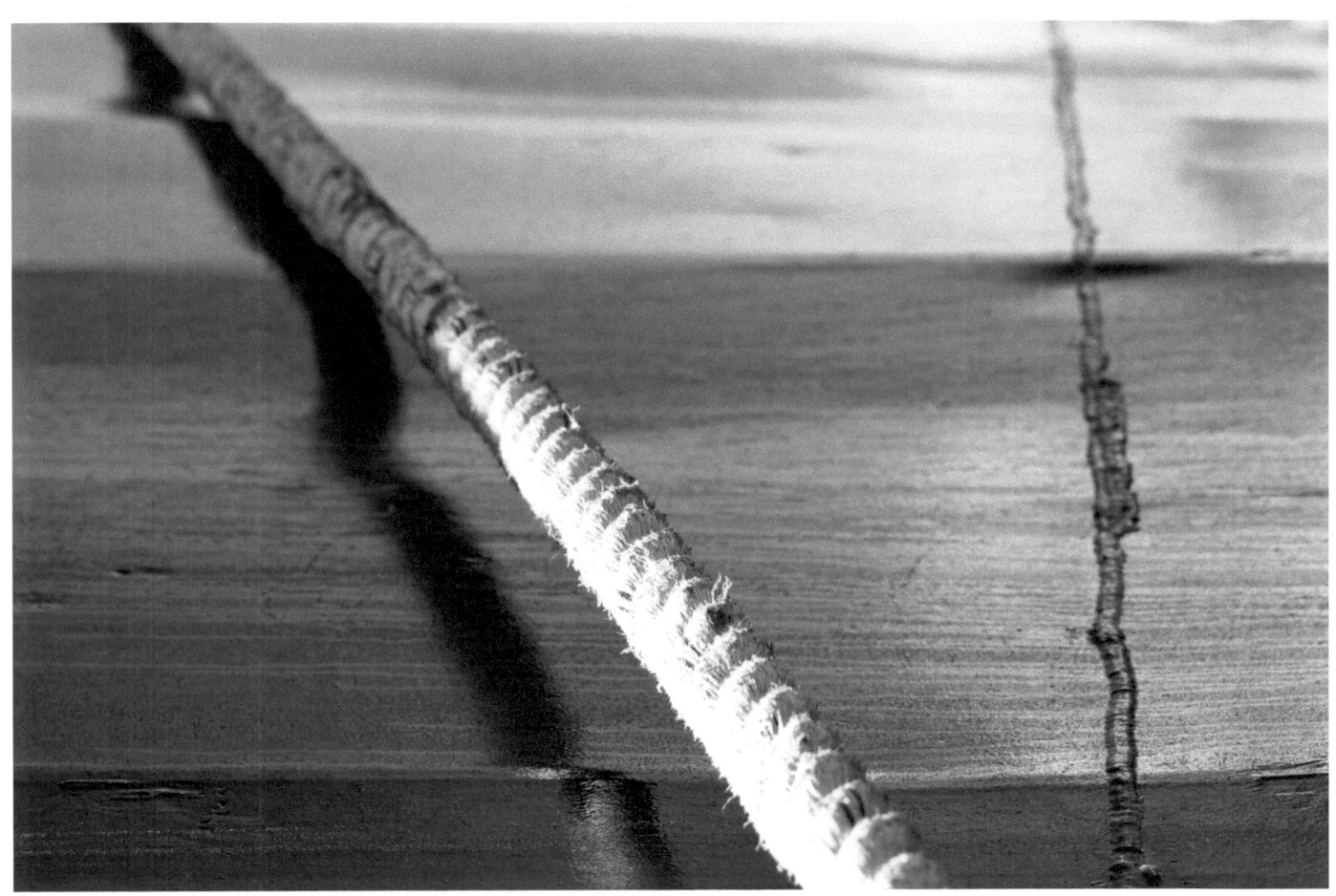

8470

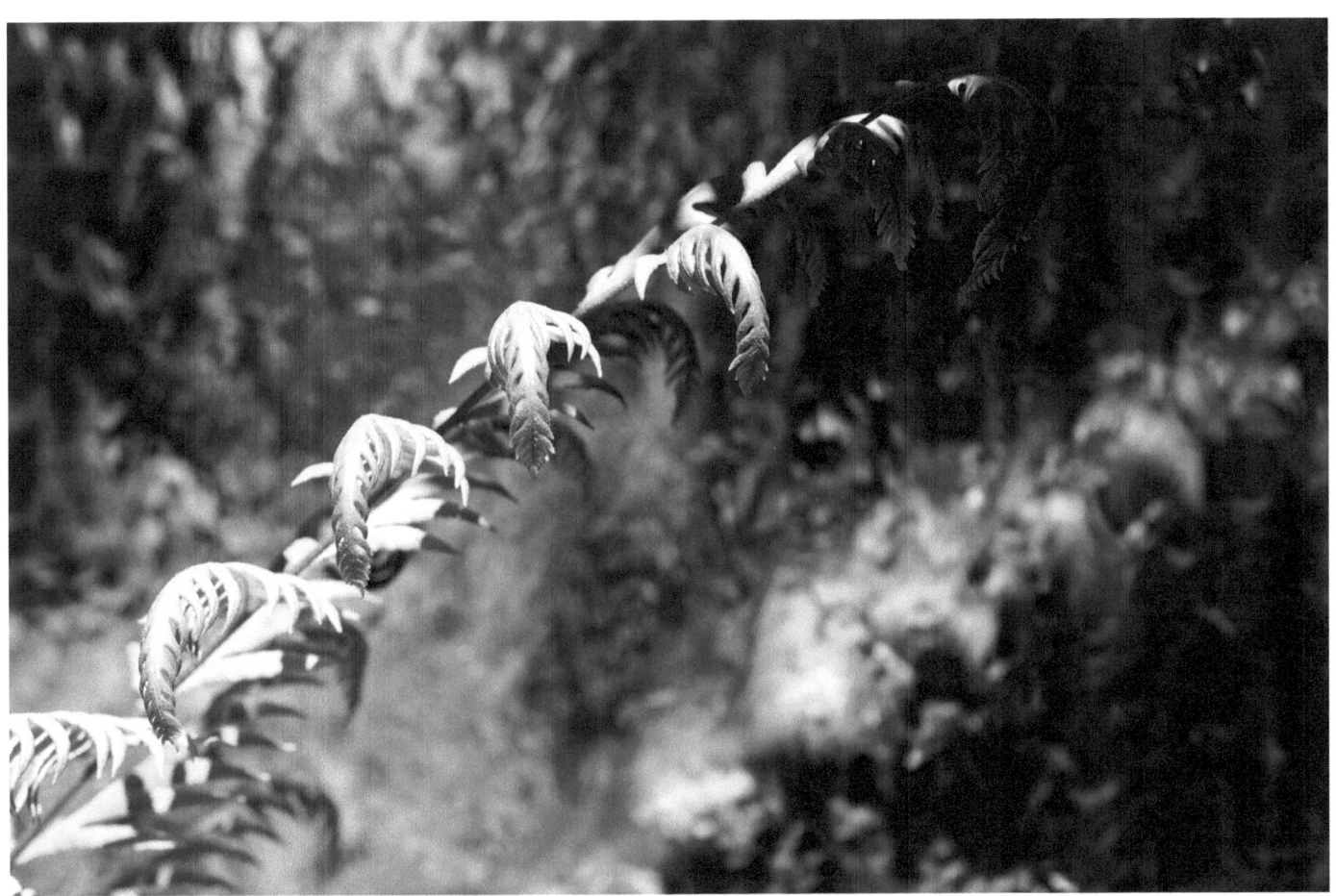

8889

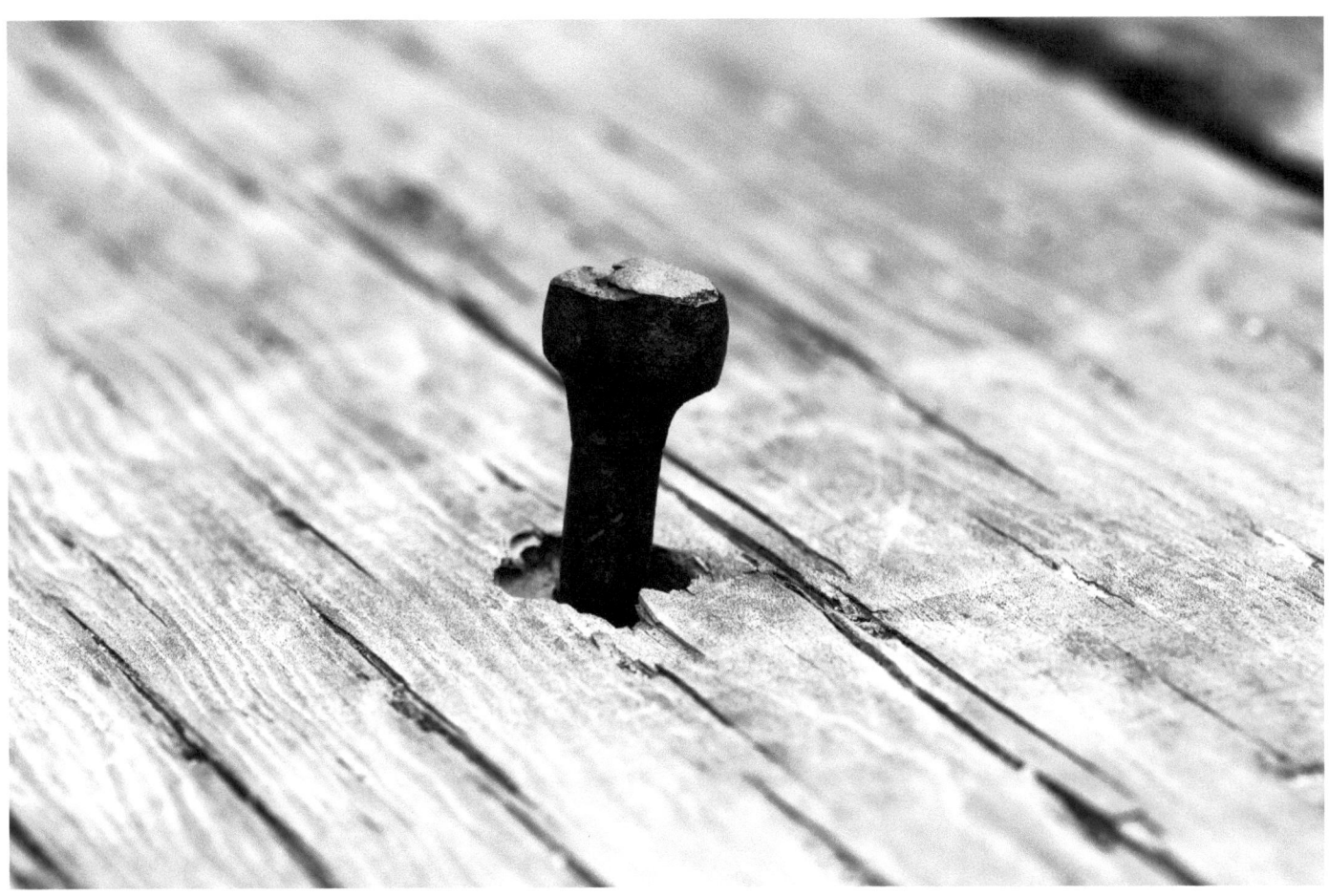

9024

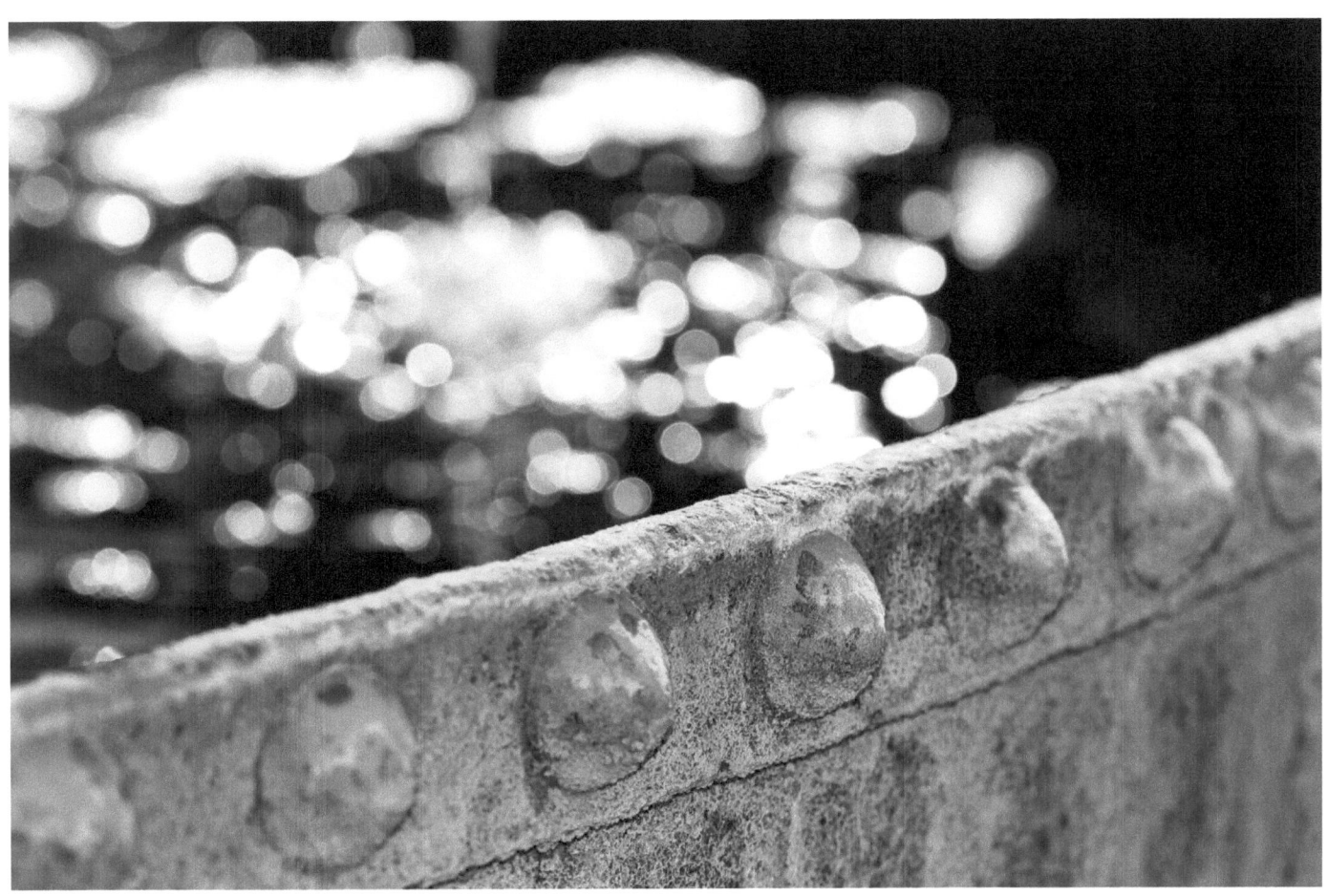

9430